D0140420

Dover Memorial Library
Gardner-Webb University
P.O. Box 836
Boiling Springs, N.C. 28017

Case Studies in Physical Education

Real World Preparation for Teaching

Edited by

Sandra A. Stroot

Holcomb Hathaway, Publishers
Scottsdale, Arizona 85250

GV
365
.C37
2000

Library of Congress Cataloging-in-Publication Data

Stroot, Sandra A.
 Case studies in physical education : real world preparation for teaching / edited by
Sandra A. Stroot.
  p.   cm.
 ISBN 1-890871-30-3
  1. Physical education and training—Study and teaching—United States—Case studies.
2. Physical education teachers—Training of—United States.   I. Title.

 GV365.S78 2000
 613.7′071′173—dc21   99-057996

Copyright © 2000 by Holcomb Hathaway, Publishers, Inc.

Holcomb Hathaway, Publishers
6207 North Cattle Track Road, Suite 5
Scottsdale, Arizona 85250
(480) 991-7881
www.hh-pub.com

10 9 8 7 6 5 4 3 2 1

ISBN 1-890871-30-3

All rights reserved. No part of this book may be
reproduced, in any form or by any means,
without permission in writing from the publisher.

Printed in the United States of America.

Contents

iii

Acknowledgments

We wish to thank the following reviewers, who read these case studies in manuscript form and offered constructive suggestions for improving them. The book is better as a result of their efforts, and we appreciate their help: Robert P. Pangrazi, Arizona State University; Mary Lou Veal, The University of North Carolina, Greensboro; Hans van der Mars, Oregon State University; and Matthew Curtner-Smith, The University of Alabama.

Using Case Methods to Explore Teaching and Learning

Sandra A. Stroot

Introduction

Welcome to the case method approach—an interesting and exciting way to explore the challenges and rewards of learning to teach. This book presents case studies based on the lives of teachers in school settings as a way to accurately reflect the world of teaching. The case studies reflect real problems encountered by educators and, as in life, there are no magic answers to the questions raised by the case studies. The purpose of this book and the case study method is not to provide you with pat answers but to help you develop the skills needed to respond to challenges you will encounter in your own teaching environment.

What Are Case Studies?

A case study is a descriptive story about real teachers in real schools (for privacy reasons, we have changed the names of the individuals in the studies). The cases illustrate situations for you to think about and talk about, and your goal will be to identify meaningful suggestions for addressing the problems. In discussing the cases, everyone will need to contribute to the learning process. Cases present a scenario, and those of you studying the case must engage in gathering and sharing information. According to Merseth (1992):

> Teachers need analytic and decision-making skills to make thoughtful assessments that induce appropriate action. Decision-making cases can hone these

1

skills. They are designed specifically to develop the power to analyze a situation, to formulate action plans, and to evaluate those actions with respect to specific context variables. (p. 53)

Using Case Methods to Explore Teaching and Learning

Teaching is a complex process that takes place in an ever-changing environment. In your methods course and other classes, you will learn many strategies to help you become a more effective teacher. The strategies, however, must be implemented in the context in which each teacher works. A particular context can make it easier or more difficult for you to apply the strategies learned in class. In addition, you will face school issues that occur outside of the gymnasium and affect your life as a teacher. This book will help you explore the issues faced by teachers in and beyond the gymnasium.

Case studies are designed to help you learn to consider and reflect. There are very few situations experienced by teachers for which there is only one "right" answer. Due to the varying needs of students, the great variety among school settings, and the complexity of the classroom, what is "right" for one student or group of students may not work with another. Because of the diverse needs of students, you, as a caring teacher, must be prepared to respond with flexibility to each situation that arises. If your first response does not work, you must be ready to respond with another option. These case studies provide opportunities to reflect on situations that are likely to occur in your school setting. They will help you explore multiple options and will better prepare you to make the appropriate choices if and when you face similar problems in the school.

These cases are not designed to be presented, interpreted, or solved by the instructor of this course. They offer you, the student reader, the opportunity to explore and solve problems through your own initiative and knowledge. At times you and your fellow students may lack the necessary knowledge to resolve an issue to your satisfaction. In such cases, you may have to gather additional information about a topic before you can provide good suggestions for addressing the problem. This parallels real life; teachers continue to learn throughout their careers, and it is important to recognize the on-going need for information gathering, peer discussion, and other forms of continuing education. For example, in order to resolve a case study, you may wish to explore similar situations in local school settings to see how teachers in your area handle similar problems. When you have analyzed scenarios and become informed about the topic, you will be prepared to make knowledgeable suggestions to solve the problem. The suggestions that you identify for solving the problems should be based on your knowledge of teaching and learning, and your knowledge of the particular topic addressed in the case.

Here are some guidelines for exploring the issues addressed in each case:

1. Before class, read through the case once. After the first reading, read through the end-of-case questions; then read through the case a second time with the questions in mind.
2. Identify all issues embedded in the case.
3. Make note of what you already know about each of these issues.
4. Begin to identify the types of information you will need to explore these scenarios and critical issues. Gather more information in areas where you have limited knowledge. Remember, you have at your fingertips Internet resources that were unimagined just a few years ago. Take advantage of the currency and availability of such information.
5. Consider courses of action to resolve the dilemma or question and consider the results of those actions.
6. Make notes on the spaces provided below the questions so you have your ideas organized and ready to share before you come to the next class.
7. In class, share the new information with your peers. Be ready to support your identification of issues and proposed solutions. You will be given opportunities to state your opinions, but you will need to provide a rationale for your choices.
8. With classmates, explore as many tangents and related issues as you can—this is meant to be a brainstorming session!
9. Identify as many solutions as possible for each issue. No one solution will be right for every context!
10. Be prepared to keep an open mind, to listen to the ideas and possible solutions offered by others, and to learn about alternate and maybe better ways to address the problem.

When you have attended to these steps during the process of reading and exploring each case, you will be well prepared for the classroom discussion. The value you derive from these discussions will be guided by the amount of effort you and your peers have put into preparation. Remember, this is not your typical lecture class. Using the case approach, you will learn to:

- Identify and explore additional resources that are pertinent to a topic.
- Analyze situations and pose solutions.
- Develop and effectively defend your point of view. As a teacher, you may be asked to provide reasons for your actions to students and administrators, and/or parents.
- Think on your feet. Keep in mind that as a teacher you will have to think quickly and respond appropriately to your students in your own classroom.
- Adapt or alter your point of view based on the ideas of your peers.

After exploring the issues embedded in the case, you will leave with multiple strategies to address many situations that may arise in your classroom. The strategy you finally use will depend on the needs of the students and the context of your own school setting.

Where Do I Get Additional Information?

There are several ways you can become more informed about a topic. First, be sure to use the textbook for your methods class to its fullest. As you probably guessed, articles from educational journals such as the *Journal of Physical Education, Recreation, and Dance, Strategies,* or *Teaching Elementary Physical Education* provide information and practical suggestions for teaching physical education. If you need research information, the *Journal of Teaching in Physical Education, Research Quarterly on Exercise and Sport,* or the *Adapted Physical Education Quarterly* are useful. Finally, the Internet is exploding with more and more valuable ideas and suggestions. When using the Internet, you might start with the PE Central site to see if this is a useful source for your specific topic: http://pe.central.vt.edu/. PE Central provides "the latest information about contemporary developmentally appropriate physical education programs for children and youth." Use this website and others to explore ideas for lesson plans and assessment, as well as information to promote and support physical education in your current and future districts. The PE Central site provides multiple links to other physical education and activity-related sites, as well as conference and workshop schedules. Users will find unlimited opportunities to explore new ideas and you will be encouraged to submit your own ideas to be published on the website.

In addition to exploring the Internet, you might go to local schools to talk with the physical education specialists. The more ideas you can bring to the table, the more information you will have to make informed choices. We suggest asking each person taking part in the classroom discussion to go to a different source and then share the information with the group.

As you gather information for the topic, brainstorm ideas and think ahead—make your best, most informed guess regarding the likely outcome of implementing each idea. Thinking the ideas through to the end helps clarify the strategies and avoid potential problems. This process is similar to creating a "flow chart"—begin by asking, "What happens if . . . ?" There is always more than one "right" answer to the problem. Explore your options so you will have choices when similar issues arise in your own classroom.

In Conclusion

These cases have been designed to address a wide variety of issues in education, including teaching methods, classroom management, multicultural education, classroom assessment, and other pertinent educational topics. In the past, case studies addressing issues and concerns of physical education specialists have not been available, and as a result, physical educators have received limited benefits from the case method approach.

These case studies are the result of the collaborative efforts of teachers and university faculty, who represent many different geographical areas in the United States. Teachers from university and school settings worked together to provide realistic case scenarios representing life in the schools from the perspective of the physical education specialists. Each case is based on real-life situations that occur in school settings, and each case represents experiences of the teachers contributing to this text.

The cases are grouped by level: high school, middle school, and elementary school. There are four cases each addressing the middle and high school levels, and eight cases focusing on issues at the elementary level. In addition, a variety of topics have been identified and pursued, including disciplinary struggles, inclusion, coworker conflict, and teaching in an urban setting, among others.

It is our hope that these cases will stimulate discussion, encourage exploration of new information, and promote critical thinking and problem-solving skills to address the issues reflected in each scenario. We hope you enjoy reading the cases, exploring new ideas, gathering additional information, and brainstorming solutions to the issues emerging in these cases. Let your imagination be your guide in this endeavor. Do not let tradition keep you from creating new, exciting ideas that can benefit you as a teacher and the students in your classes.

Coworker Conflict

Kathy LaMaster

Kimerly Call

M. B. Seasons

Case

1

I
t was early Monday morning as Sally Worthingway entered the school building. Sally walked down empty locker-lined hallways to the gymnasium and into the physical education equipment room. She treasured this time before school when the gymnasium was quiet and she could organize her equipment and prepare for the day's lessons. Since school began two months ago, this had become her time to think and enjoy her work atmosphere without the presence of Bill Thompson, her coworker. Graduating with honors the previous year from State University allowed her to select from the best job openings. It was Sally's first year as a physical education teacher and coach. Positive experiences in physical activity had impacted her career decision. She anticipated teaching students to enjoy activity and develop healthy lifestyles through physical education classes. She wanted to be a positive role model to her students.

Trinity High School was a suburban school located in an affluent district where 95 percent of the school's population of 1,500 students were Caucasians. College preparatory classes were the academic focus to the extent that vocational classes were not even offered. A graduation rate of 92 percent or higher, with the majority of students attending nationally known universities, was achieved yearly.

Sally remembered her eighteenth birthday celebration with great fondness. Was Sally naïve to think that times had not changed? Even if things were different for teens now than they had been for her, there was still the violation of the substance abuse policy, and in the presence of a coach.

As a reflection of community pride and tradition, Trinity High School excelled in both academics and athletics.

The position at Trinity was a dream job with a good salary, representing an opportunity of a lifetime. During the summer interview process, answers to questions concerning the existing curriculum led Sally to believe that the physical education program was one of excellence. In fact, on the day she interviewed she was shown a large, well-stocked equipment room and facilities available for physical education. Descriptions of physical education classes had depicted well-organized activities involving high student participation. Now as a teacher at Trinity High School, Sally realized that the high-quality program she was led to believe existed there was an illusion. Her coworker, Bill, did not focus on teaching skills. He did, however, like the students to have a good time in class. Sally was determined to make the physical education program more credible. She wanted to make a difference!

Bill had worked at Trinity High School for fifteen years and put more effort into coaching athletic teams than teaching physical education classes. Typically he would arrive in the gym just as the first bell was sounding and ask Sally what she had planned for the day. From Sally's perspective, Bill liked to team teach because he could work on his practice plans or game statistics. Bill coached the varsity boys' basketball team, and they had been in the final four state tournament for six of the past eight years. Last year the team was undefeated until the final game, where they lost in a last-second shot that rolled around the inside rim prior to popping out of the hoop. This was the year! All starters were returning, including an All-State player, and preseason polls ranked Trinity first.

Sally had enjoyed competitive sports as a two-season athlete in high school and college. However, she did not understand how Bill could think so little of his role as physical educator and was amazed how he had maintained his teaching job for so many years. It was common knowledge among faculty members that Bill was having family problems and had been arrested for driving under the influence of alcohol twice in the past year. His school duties had also been impacted as he had become negligent concerning the grading his physical education classes. At the end of each semester he would just mimeograph his roster and write "all A's" at the top, then place it in the homeroom teachers' boxes.

"Hi, Ms. Worthingway. What are you doing?" Sally jumped as Rick, a student, interrupted her thoughts.

"Hi, Rick, I'm getting ready for our class today. Aren't you running just a bit early? School doesn't start for another thirty minutes," Sally teased Rick.

Rick was a student in Sally's first-period class. He was a quiet, tall senior, and had just been selected as cocaptain on the varsity basketball team. The importance of the upcoming basketball season was paramount, as several colleges would be watching the team to see Rick's teammate, Mark, who was Trinity's All-District, All-State basketball player. Mark had established new school records during the past season as the lacrosse team goalie. He was also cocaptain and star of the varsity basketball team. Last year had also been great for Rick, having been selected to the All-District team. However, his season-ending shot, which rolled out of the basket, had left him with the reputation of choking under pressure.

Sally and Rick had developed a good relationship throughout the past couple of months. Sally enjoyed Rick's presence in the physical education classroom because he always encouraged the other students to participate and modeled fair play with all of his peers. Sally was really pleased that he was going to be cocaptain of the basketball team and she believed Rick would be a great team leader.

Rick shifted his feet and dug his hands deep into the pockets of his faded blue jeans. "I was wondering if you had a moment to talk?" Then he quickly added, "I'll come back if this is a bad time," and started to turn away.

Sally reached out and touched his arm. "Rick, I always make time for students. Let's go to my office and talk." She remembered her school days and how teachers had been positive role models. Her parents were both high-powered corporate executives and had made it quite clear that they had little time in the evenings for listening to her "childish" school problems. As a result, Sally had been left to work out the dilemmas of youth on her own or with her friends. Her physical education teachers had also been a great influence on her development as a person. They had instilled in her the importance of integrity, loyalty, and honesty. In college, Sally had been quickly identified as a great listener, and her peers in the dorm frequently knocked on her door with their problems. Now she had the opportunity to make an impact with students and was not going to turn her back if someone needed to talk.

Once they had moved to the office, it became apparent that Rick was struggling with a big problem. Throughout the previous months she had come to recognize Rick as an easy-going student, but now he was seated rigidly in his chair and was definitely nervous. From earlier experiences Sally had learned that it was best to patiently wait for the other person to begin rather than ask questions. After a few moments, Rick began to share his story with Sally. As the story progressed, Sally became more uncomfortable with her coworker, Coach Bill Thompson.

According to Rick, on the previous Friday evening Mark's parents had thrown him an eighteenth birthday party. Coach Thompson had been jokingly asked by a few players at basketball practice on Friday to "drop by" and help celebrate, so it surprised Rick to see Coach at the party. Rick had also been shocked that a keg of beer had been available since the consumption of alcohol contradicted the school district's substance-abuse policy. This policy did not allow students involved in extracurricular activities to consume or be in the company of those consuming alcoholic beverages at any time during the school year. Violation of this policy could result in a suspension from the current athletic team and loss of any leadership role. Players did have the option of "self-reporting" to any school official, which would allow for leniency on a first offense.

As Rick recalled the evening's events, he related that shortly after arriving, he decided to make an excuse and remove himself from the situation. However, Mark's parents and Coach Thompson had encouraged him to stay and have some pizza that had been ordered. When the pizza arrived, three boxes were carried into the living room by a female delivery person. It was at this time that the delivery person opened her phony pizza boxes, turned on a tape recorder, and began a strip-tease performance. Rick was stunned and quickly glanced around the room to observe his peers' reactions. Many of his teammates and Coach Thompson were making rude and provocative calls and reaching for dollar bills to sustain the entertainment. Coach Thompson proceeded to demonstrate to the players the correct way of awarding the dancer a dollar bill. It was at this point that Rick went home. Rick had spent the remainder of the weekend confused about the effect this would have on him, the team, and also the school. He was positive that the rumors would start early Monday morning and he did not want to be implicated in the situation. The upcoming basketball season was going to be his chance for a college scholarship.

After Rick finished his story, Sally did not know how to respond to his account of the events. She told him that she needed to think about the situation and would have to get back to him after some thought. Rick thanked her for her time and left the office. Coach Thompson was unlocking his office door and glanced up as Rick was exiting Sally's office.

Later that evening, Sally sat on the couch sipping a hot cup of tea, looking out the window at the falling rain. She was reflecting on the events of the day. She was mentally and physically exhausted! In her lap lay the slip of paper she had found in her teacher mailbox as she left school. Her classes had progressed as planned, but she did not feel satisfaction with her job as a teacher on this day. Her thoughts had continuously returned to the conversation with Rick. She wondered what she could do. Sally had attended parties when she was a teenager. She remembered her eighteenth birthday celebration with great fondness. Several of her friends had helped her commemorate the important transition from youth to adulthood, but they had celebrated in a different way. Was Sally naïve to think that times had not changed? Even if things were different for teens now than they had been for her, there was still the violation of the substance-abuse policy and in the presence of a coach. Throughout the entire day she had felt uneasy around Bill. She was troubled by her perceptions and lack of respect for him as a teacher. Glancing down, she was reminded of the single slip of paper from the principal simply stating, "Meet me in my office tomorrow at 7:45 A.M." Sally shivered.

Name   Date

Questions
Preparing for Learning & Teaching

1. What is the critical issue in this case?

2. Who are the main characters in the case?

3. What do you think Sally should do with the information from Rick? And when?

4. Should Sally have gone directly to Bill to hear his side of the story or to confront him?

5. What should Sally tell Rick?

6. Does the fact that Sally is a first-year teacher impact her response?

7. If a coach/teacher knowingly violates a school policy, what should be the consequences?

8. If action is taken with the coach and/or basketball team, what should it be? If action is taken, should Rick be excused from the action?

9. Problem solve for each main character: Sally, Rick, and Bill. Identify their responsibility following this event.

10. What other strategies might you use to address these issues?

11. What are some of the related issues and questions raised by this case?

12. What are some of the possible reasons that the principal has asked Sally to come to his office? If possible, role-play the various scenarios and discuss possible outcomes.

Team Leadership

Pamela Bechtel

Mary O'Sullivan

Reggie Oliver

Case 2

As Tony slumped into the chair in his physical education office, the only thoughts he acknowledged were "What have I gotten myself into? It all seemed to be so simple and it worked so well at the workshop. What has happened to change everything? Why wasn't my class going the way they said it would? Maybe I don't really know what I am trying to do." All of these thoughts raced through his head as he reflected back on his last class of the day.

Tony had been teaching physical education for several years at an urban high school in the Midwest. He was always open to trying new curricular approaches and teaching strategies to keep his physical education classes exciting and relevant to his students' lives. He had attended a workshop on the Sport Education Model for middle and high school students in the fall, and now it was January and he was trying to incorporate this curriculum approach into his program. As he had learned in the workshop, the Sport Education Model is a curriculum and instruction model that provides more authentic sport experiences than the more traditional physical education curriculum model. Students play on the same team through the season, and they also have responsibilities for coaching, scoring, refereeing, and keeping player statistics during their physical education program.

Today, her team was arguing over their warm-up routine, which still hadn't been decided. This aggravated the underlying dissension among the team members, which had begun earlier with their discussions about their choice for a team name. Tony finally went over to Joelle's team, seeing little that resembled the practice task the captains were supposed to be leading.

13

Tony liked using the Sport Education Model, and he was using it in his four classes during the day. Only one class seemed to be having a problem. But what was the reason Sport Education wasn't working as well with this class as with the other classes? What was different between third and fourth period? He could think of nothing at the moment. He just couldn't figure out why two of his five teams were not getting the tasks completed. He knew that the participation levels of these two teams were much lower than the other three teams. "Did I tell them anything that was different in our team captains' meeting?" He thought for a moment and then recalled that he had told every class the same thing. He recalled the lesson where he explained how students in a Sport Education program needed to take some leadership for their class. He remembered he had told them they "would be working in teams and would need captains who had the following qualities: (1) they wanted to be a captain, (2) they were ready and willing to assume a leadership role, and (3) they knew what it meant to be a team leader. He had even made sure he gave each one a handout that included the roles and responsibilities of being a team captain. Nothing seemed to have been left out. In each class he had reviewed these key points and had asked for a raise of hands from those students who wanted to be captains. He then selected five students, trying to include both males and females as captains. He made sure each prospective captain read the handout and understood his or her responsibilities. Before the next class, all captains had met with Tony, and each captain had randomly selected five cards, each containing the name of a student in their class; these five names made up their teams. He thought he had followed the suggestions made on team and captain selection at the workshop, but this class had two teams that just were not functioning as Tony thought they should. "What was different about these two teams?" he wondered.

Clarence and Joelle were captains of the teams that were not functioning well. Clarence's team was refusing to do much of anything that he suggested. Joelle's team seemed clueless as to what to do next, as she provided little sense of direction or guidance to her teammates.

Clarence was very athletic, but due to family responsibilities, he had to get a job after school and did not have time to both work and participate in athletics. He had been active on the football and track teams during middle school and his first year in high school. Clarence's team never seemed to listen to him. Lately they had started to listen more to one of the other team members rather than to Clarence. In fact, Clarence's team created a commotion each day when it was time for the captain to go through the day's plan. At this stage, no one was paying attention to Clarence or his directions. He was always yelling at them, "Follow my directions and practice it the way I said. No—I said you have to do it this way." The low point came when Clarence belittled one of the members on his team by telling her that he wished he had never chosen her because, as he put it, "You're a loser!" That really set the girl off, and Tony had to intervene for fear that Clarence would face a mutiny by his teammates. The girl, Annie, had asked Tony to let her go to a new team, but Tony had said no. In his conversation with Annie, he had told her she would need to talk to the rest of the team and they would have to work this out together. He had said that switching teams wouldn't really help the team deal with the problem they had.

Joelle's team was another story. When Tony had asked for volunteers to fill the role of captain at the beginning of the Sport Education volleyball season, Joelle's hand had been the first one in the air. Even after he had handed out the information sheet describing the responsibilities and expectations of a captain, she had sought the role and accepted it without question. Tony didn't recall Joelle having been a strong leader in the past, but he wanted females as captains, so he jumped at the chance when Joelle showed an interest. Today, her team was arguing over their warm-up routine, which still hadn't been decided. This aggravated the underlying dissension among the team members, which had begun earlier with their discussions about their choice for a team name. Tony overheard Joelle telling her team, "Come on, you guys, you need to underhand toss the ball to one player and they need to pass it to the target. It doesn't matter what pass you do, just get it back to the target. You can have as many people working together as you want and switch when the tosser is tired." Tony finally went over to Joelle's team, seeing little that resembled the practice task the captains were supposed to be leading. Some were forearm passing, some overhead passing, and some just tossing the ball around. Tony decided it was time for him to take charge, and he set them up in their triad formation and explained the practice task to the team. During this intervention, Tony encouraged Joelle to assist him with the practice. She, however, just stood there watching her teammates, never giving any feedback to them or providing any directions for them to follow. This had been the problem for several class periods, but he had not intervened before today.

After this lesson, Tony had wondered whether or not he had provided enough relevant information to the captains to practice the tasks. Or were the problems he observed with Joelle and Clarence specific to them? Before the practice time each day Tony called all of the captains over and told them exactly how to set up and run the drill. Today he had explained the drill for forearm passing in triads and what the skill progression would be. He had written this out on a task card for each team so the captains could take it back to their practice area and use it as a guide for their team practices. He had done this for every class since the beginning of the volleyball season.

Tony had to admit that there definitely were some problems, not with the teams' members but rather with their captains. He knew that in the Sport Education Model you needed to have captains, but now he wished he had spent more time deciding who would be captain, as it seemed this was a key issue in the success of the model with high school students. All of the captains that Tony had chosen had told him they could fulfill their new role with their classmates. Tony thought that Clarence knew he couldn't boss his team members but that he had to be respectful, even when they upset him or didn't participate to his expectations. Tony was sure Joelle realized that she needed to be a stronger captain by giving more detailed directions, but she hadn't demonstrated this at all this season.

What was he to do now? Would he choose new captains for those teams? Would he hold individual conferences with Clarence and Joelle to discuss his concerns, or would he just leave things as they were until the end of the season and then make sure they were not captains next season? He wished now he had been more attentive to how best to deal with this component of the Sport Education Model, but he had to act now. He decided to think about his options and make his decision before he saw this class the next day.

Name   Date

Preparing for Learning & Teaching

1. What is the critical issue in this case?

2. What does Tony feel the role of a volleyball captain should be according to his understanding of the Sport Education Model?

3. From Tony's perspective, what is the problem? What are the captains doing or not doing that bothers him?

4. What benefits does Tony believe the use of the Sport Education Model will provide to his classes?

5. What are other appropriate methods for selecting captains and teams in physical education? Which would you suggest that Tony consider utilizing when the next opportunity for captain and team selection occurs?

6. Should the selection of appropriate captains be a concern when using the Sport Education Model? Why or why not?

7. What option(s) does Tony have in dealing with the captains who are having problems with their teams?

8. How might teachers assess the leadership abilities of their captains?

9. What role might students have in choosing a leader? What might be some advantages of having students involved in this process? The disadvantages?

10. What might teachers do to help students learn to take on leadership roles?

11. Are there different effective leadership styles, and if so, which one(s) would be most appropriate for your physical education program?

12. What are some of the related issues and questions raised by this case?

13. What strategies might you use to address these issues?

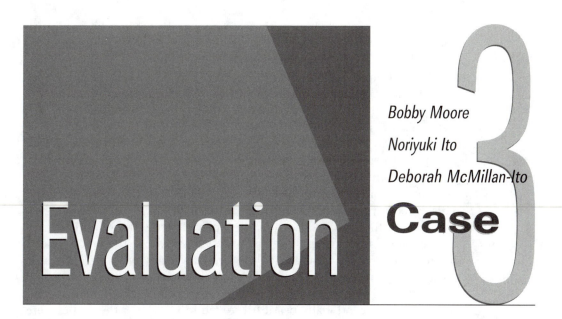

Bobby Moore

Noriyuki Ito

Deborah McMillan-Ito

Evaluation

Case 3

Wandering down the hall in a perplexed daze, Ken mentally rehashed the entire frustrating meeting. He thought about how Roy's pudgy pointer finger had sounded when it hammered on the table. He remembered Barbara's bobbing head as it bounced from the sports page to the conversation and back again. They were supposed to be educators. Why couldn't they understand? His suspicions had been confirmed, and Ken was now certain that his proposed change of the current evaluation system would receive little, if any, support from his coworkers. He wondered how they could remain so adamantly against improvement of the physical education program. Arriving at his office, he sat down at his desk and looked out the window. Ken thought to himself, "At least Cantor is backing me." Ken remembered his first days at the school and the responsibility conferred upon him by Mr. Cantor, the principal, for bringing a renewed sense of credibility to the physical education department.

A little over a year had passed since Ken Brewster started working at Arthur T. Bennington High School in New Stoughton. His first teaching position as a physical educator had been at Meadowbrook High School, an upper middle-class school that was considered a pleasant place to teach. Ken's hard work, initiative, proven interest, and competency in the field of physical education had earned him a reputation as an excellent

Roy King had remained adamant with Ken about his position, stating that implementation of the letter-grade system was opening up a Pandora's box. He argued, "There is nothing at all wrong with the current system. The kids are good. The parents are happy. Why are you trying to fix something that's not broken?"

educator. Although he had initially enjoyed this position, he found the course work and research that his master's degree courses offered to be far more stimulating and challenging.

After completing his master's degree and five years of service at Meadowbrook, Ken was offered a job in New Stoughton, an extremely affluent suburb located just outside the largest city in the state. Mr. Cantor had heard of Ken's demonstrated commitment to improving physical education at Meadowbrook, and of his familiarity with current educational theories in physical education. It was for those reasons that Mr. Cantor had hired Ken. On Ken's first day at school, Mr. Cantor enthusiastically welcomed him into his office and said, "Welcome to Bennington. This school's physical education department needs an aspiring, progressive teacher like you. It also needs a renewed sense of credibility. I recommended you for the position because I think you're the one who can improve the program. I'm looking forward to working with you." Ken was flattered, and repeated to himself, "A renewed sense of credibility."

New Stoughton was an immaculate town. Ken quickly became accustomed to the exceptionally beautiful surroundings. All of the homes were well preserved but the newer ones were stunning. Ninety-four percent of New Stoughton's inhabitants were upper class. Parents held high expectations for themselves, their community, and their children. All of the schools in the town excelled academically. It was assumed by Bennington's students, parents, and teachers that graduating students would continue their education at a university. The only uncertainty left for students to ponder prior to graduation was to which universities they would submit their applications. The community not only held high academic expectations for the town's schools, but also expected students to excel in extracurricular activities, particularly athletics. A regularly circulated rumor in New Stoughton stated that the length of time a coach remained at the school was directly proportional to his or her win–loss record. The teams from New Stoughton's schools regularly placed either first or second in their athletic conference. Bennington High was no exception. The facilities, which included a swimming pool, a gymnasium equipped with three basketball courts and a racquetball court, five tennis courts, an archery net, and other state-of-the-art equipment, not only ensured Bennington's success within their athletic conference but also provided the physical educators, Roy King, Barbara Allen, and Ken, with an unsurpassed environment in which to teach physical education. Teachers with positions at schools that were understaffed, whose facilities were less than adequate, whose parents were less than approachable, or where students were unmotivated would find this school an educational oasis.

New Stoughton parents themselves were highly educated and respected professionals in their fields, who understood the long-term importance of a high-quality education. They actively participated in their children's education from preschool until graduation from college. Both students and parents were extremely aware of the correlation between high grade-point averages and admittance into a highly respected university. Parents and their children focused on high grade-point averages (GPA) long before the students entered Bennington. By the time these young adults arrived at Bennington, this preoccupation with GPA and academic achievement had thoroughly rooted itself and become part of their culture. As a result of their deep respect for education and the degree of importance they granted it, the parents were adamant, demanding, and vocal with regard to the rigorous curriculum and the evaluation systems employed by educators. The parents of Bennington's students understood that their expectations were high and so suitably equipped the school's financial coffers to enable the teachers to perform their jobs well.

Initially Ken was extremely impressed with the students. They were highly motivated and concentrated on succeeding in academic courses; therefore, there were very few discipline problems. Few students were enrolled in study halls, which were perceived as opportunities missed. Several students considered their lunch hour an optional study period during which they chose to attend a class such as band or orchestra, rather than squander away the time in the cafeteria. Students were aggressive, determined learners, yet their fervor for learning had rarely manifested itself in Ken's earlier physical education classes. In his first months at Bennington, Ken often wondered how, in a school filled with so many bright, highly motivated individuals, active in intramural and interscholastic sports, his physical education classes could be filled with large numbers of apathetic, unmotivated kids. Ken occasionally overheard students' conversations about physical education class.

"Have you studied? I've got gym sixth period, and I'm going to study for chemistry then."

"Gross! I hate it when I dress up and then have to change for gym. You get all sweaty."

"Yeah. And your hair feels gross. P. E. is just like second-grade recess! I just asked my mother to write a note excusing me from gym. She says I shouldn't exert myself. If I get hot and sweaty, I can hardly concentrate in the classes that really count. I've got to get an 'A' in chemistry."

Ken found it insulting when students chose not to participate in a physical education class in order to study for a chemistry or any other test. Roy King, on the other hand, excused the students, wished them luck, and sent them on their way to huddle with their chemistry book. Roy was a genuinely likable person, but as a coworker and professional he was infuriating. Roy King's personality and style of teaching were all from the "old school." Actually, school didn't figure into the formula, because he used very few of the newer concepts and theories available to current educators. Ken saw that almost all of the other educators were constantly reevaluating their programs and participating in staff development. Instructors in other areas were developing strategies for authentic assessment and cooperative learning based on new trends in education. Yet the physical education department continued to offer the same musty program combined with the same dated method of evaluation based on a student's attitude, dress, and participation. It was this style of teaching and attitude that had long since transformed physical education classes at Bennington into recess periods. Whenever the topic of revision of evaluation standards was brought up, Roy reminded Ken that only 22 months and 7 days stood between him and retirement. Roy often said he wanted to enjoy his last months of teaching, and implementation of Ken's new evaluation system would effectively erase that idea. Roy was, if nothing else, genuine and honest with his opinions.

Roy King had good rapport with the parents. Indeed, he should. He had been teaching at Bennington for almost 23 years. He had been there so long that he was now teaching some of his original students' children. Bennington had changed over the years, and Roy King had seen and lived through the changes. During the course of his career, Roy had also, on several occasions, attempted to implement his own theories and programs. He had seen other physical educators enter the school with their grandiose plans and ideas. "Some," he often pointed out to Ken, "succeeded brilliantly, while the majority took nosedives only to crash and burn."

On several occasions, Roy referred to Ken's new evaluation system as completely ridiculous. Roy spoke from experience. He had taught for a period of time using letter grades as the form of evaluation. The pressure exerted on him and the other physical educators in the school by students and their parents to "adjust" grades, which had already been recorded on report cards, had been tremendous. Students complained every term. "Hearing complaints is a part of teaching," Roy said. "Students accustomed to receiving A's, but who unfortunately earned B's or C's in physical education class, took their complaints home. The grades appeared unfair or unjust to parents. These were parents who had been grooming their child for college since before the child was able to walk. Grade-point averages are everything here. I was never able to adjust to manipulative parents and administrators, especially principals. It was degrading to have my judgment not only questioned but overridden by someone who had not seen how the child actually performed in the class. Every term parents and students complained vehemently about the grades." Roy said he had become so tired of being overridden by principals and having to change grades that when the administration decided to endorse and revert to the pass/fail evaluation system for physical education, he was extremely relieved. Overjoyed was the word, which Roy punctuated with hand gestures to describe his feelings on that day, years earlier, when the letter-grade evaluation system was reversed. Roy's tirade against Ken's new unit, based on a letter-grade evaluation system and student accountability, invariably began with his description of the deep-seated frustration he held with principals and ended with a summation of days left until his retirement. Roy made his opinion perfectly clear. Barbara Allen, on the other hand, always kept her opinions about the revision proposal carefully shrouded by reading the sports section of the newspaper.

Ken knew that Barbara Allen was just as averse to the new evaluation system as Roy. Barbara, however, had not been as graphic and outspoken as Roy when discussion focused on revision of the evaluation system and the experimental units Ken had developed. Ken almost felt more comfortable with Roy's outright criticism of the unit than with the unstated contempt that Barbara seemed to have developed for him. Barbara Allen had taught with Roy King for a decade. She had been hired directly upon graduating from college. She wanted to avoid the evaluation revision issue. Actually, she wanted to avoid Ken. The work environment had been comfortable until he was hired. Barbara had originally felt relieved when she was informed that another physical educator had been hired. An additional physical education teacher, she assumed, meant that she would be responsible for fewer classes. She thought Ken would help lessen the pressures she was feeling, but instead he seemed to be threatening to compound them. Though Ken hadn't realized it, his enthusiastic and aggressive attempt at reform had inadvertently offended Barbara. Barbara saw Ken as someone ignorant of the unstated rules of hierarchy based on seniority, who was treading in restricted areas. Ken was the new person. Barbara was sometimes amazed at his inability to recognize that fact. She sometimes wondered what supernatural power had magically conferred Ken with a status usually afforded a teacher having ten years' experience, thereby elevating him to a level beyond greenhorn. She felt frustrated by the fact that Ken often initially discussed changes in the physical education program with Mr. Cantor. Roy was the person who first told Barbara about these meetings. Her mind jumped to the old comedic question and she half seriously asked Roy, "What are you and I? Chopped liver?" It took her only a few seconds to evaluate her reputation as a coach and her basketball teams' winning records. "No," was the answer and the word that often came to mind in association with Ken and his proposals. While she believed the revision would be helpful and would possibly motivate the students to actively participate in class, her professional interests did not lie in pursuing this program revision.

Barbara, in fact, coached one of the most successful teams in New Stoughton, the girls' varsity basketball team. In recent years, the girls' basketball team had gained a following almost equal to that of Bennington's male team. The team enjoyed great support from the community and had a winning tradition. This tradition was no accident. It was the result of Barbara's enormous investment of time and energy. Bennington was a fine school in which to teach. Students rarely caused disruptions or problems. It had always been a pleasure to work with Roy King. Bennington had provided Barbara a relatively stress-free job, which gave her time to concentrate on coaching.

In this morning's meeting with the physical education staff, Roy had remained adamant about his position, stating that implementation of the letter-grade system was opening up a Pandora's box. He argued, "There is nothing at all wrong with the current system. The kids are good. The parents are happy. Why are you trying to fix something that's not broken?" He had hammered his pointer finger on the table as he enunciated, "Leave it alone." He warned that if such an evaluation system were ever implemented on a school-wide basis, lots of parents and students would regularly, every six weeks, be thrown into an uproar. "Some have already called! And next there'll be Cantor. Save yourself, buddy!" Ken didn't completely understand the meaning of the comments, but knew Roy wanted no part in revamping the system, at least not until after 22 months and 7 days had passed. Barbara thought that by arguing against the new system she would somehow be validating it as a concept. She chose to negate it and Ken's existence by ignoring both and reading the newspaper. Ken assumed Barbara had little interest in his plan to revise the evaluation system for she had never shown any form of support for the idea. She was dragging her feet out of apparent loyalty to Roy and in mourning for the ideal coaching situation that might be jeopardized with this program revision.

Roy, Ken thought, had not noticed how well the implementation had been researched and planned. To allay his frustration with Roy's and Barbara's attitudes, Ken reminded himself of the mission entrusted to him by Mr. Cantor. Ken knew there would be resistance from parents, as Roy had warned, but he felt confident in the ultimate outcome. Ken was in a different position than Roy had been. Not only was Mr. Cantor encouraging the evaluation revision and utilization of the test units, he held the expectation that Ken would ultimately be the one who would bring credibility to the physical education department. Even if the other physical educators were resistant to change, Ken felt that with the support of the principal, he could slowly begin to develop and implement a new grading system, one that would motivate the students.

Mr. Cantor had concurred with Ken's ideas for revising the evaluation system and encouraged him to work on a proposal and materials that would help him implement the new system. Ken's goal had been to test and develop a new physical education program, based on student accountability using a letter-grade based evaluation system. Thus far the program had been a tremendous success. Ken was looking forward to collaborating with Mr. Cantor. The two had agreed that, in the near future, they would present Ken's letter-grade based program to the school's decision makers and propose its large-scale implementation.

Mr. Cantor confided in Ken that he believed the other physical educators, over an extended period of time, had become frustrated with students' apathetic attitude but had learned to tolerate and even accept it. The teachers' attitude fed off those of the students, and the students' attitude fed off those of the teachers. This was the reason, Mr. Cantor concluded, why students had come to find physical education such a stale, dispensable class. Ken had only known Mr. Cantor for a little over a year, but Ken liked being the person in the physical education department with whom the principal entrusted his observations.

The bell rang and forced Ken to end his deliberations over Roy, Barbara, and this morning's differences of opinion. He walked to the gymnasium where he set up the nets to play volleyball. Three students, Shelly Lawrence, Griffin Smolsk, and Phil Marrow, had, over the past semester, developed a habit of submitting notes to Ken from their parents excusing them from physical education class. Shelly and Phil were both healthy high school students involved in intramural sports. Their parents were among a small group who, believing that their children's participation in an intramural sport should suffice for physical education credit, requested that their children be excused from the regular physical education classes. State law did not allow for this, but the parents were extremely aggressive and took their complaints to the school board and other members of the administration. Mr. Cantor had explained to Roy, Barbara, and Ken that while those parents' actions would never be condoned, central office administrators had made the suggestion to overlook the occasional nonparticipation of these students in physical education class. Ken at first found this to be extremely grating but had, with time, become accustomed to it. Shelly and Phil often chose to use the period to review for a test, or to quiz each other for the college entrance examination. They never disrupted the class. Griffin was not an athletically inclined person. Although he enjoyed helping Ken organize the class, he didn't enjoy participating in physical education and particularly disliked sports that involved teamwork. For these reasons, during units he found particularly unpleasant, he came to class with a note from his father excusing him from physical education.

Shortly after the bell had rung, pairs and small groups of students entered the gym. A few had remained unaffected by Ken's revised units. Upon entering the gym those students immediately plopped themselves on the floor. Others who had previously been in that group were responding positively to Ken's revised units and began performing warm-up drills on their own. Ken was happy to see how the program had motivated some students to take a proactive role in physical education class.

At the beginning of the semester, Ken had implemented his new evaluation system and the revised units. He continued to test his new system in a volleyball unit. Ken first familiarized the students with the subject of volleyball and explained how they would be assessed in this unit. He explained that, while they would still receive a pass or fail grade on their report card, he would calculate their grades based on the objectives they met. This letter grade would reflect what they actually earned in the class. He would make these grades available to students by posting them on his office door. As in all of his new units, he gave each student a list of objectives that included a variety of goals based on skills, knowledge, understanding of the rules, and even peer-teaching, in which students were required to teach a skill to a fellow classmate. The students worked diligently to perfect their passing, hitting, and serving skills. The students had been required to pass a rules test before they could participate in a volleyball game. Ken began to notice something he had not seen in his classes before. Students worked and practiced hard to develop efficient skills. They were also working together productively. They were even utilizing charts on the wall, which Ken had made for them to keep track of their objectives. During the fourth week of this unit, the students were playing modified volleyball games and developing team strategies. Though this had been the outcome he had hoped for, Ken often found himself amazed at how skilled the students had become in such a short period of time. He was also amazed by how many students actively participated, and how much their attitude toward physical education class had changed. In this, the sixth and last week of the unit, the students were participating in volleyball games. The students were sincere in their efforts and played hard. Ken was impressed with the students and proud of the new evaluation program.

During the last grading period when Ken evaluated the objectives and outcomes of each student, he noted that out of his class of 24 students, 15 had received A's, 5 had received B's, and 1 had received a C. It was fortunate for Shelly, Phil, and Griffin that the school had not adopted Ken's new evaluation system, for under it they would not have passed physical education class. These were fair assessments, Ken thought. If a student completed only 80 percent of the objectives, they would receive a B.

Even though Ken had to assign a pass/fail grade on the students' report cards, he felt the new system motivated and challenged more of the students than the old system. At the end of the first six weeks, many students had come to check the roster posted on Ken's door to see what they would have received on their report card had they been assessed on the basis of a letter-grade evaluation system. Ken, in developing and implementing the new letter-grade based program, discovered a new excitement and a sense of pride in teaching. He had thoroughly enjoyed the volleyball unit and was truly looking forward to the start of next week's floor hockey unit. He hadn't felt this way about classes for a long time.

As Ken began the trek to his office through the crowded hall, he saw Barbara. He thought she had looked his way and, in hopes of lessening what seemed to be an intense dislike for him, Ken responded with a nod of acknowledgment and a big toothy grin. Evidently he had been mistaken. Perhaps she hadn't seen him. If she did, she chose not to respond. Upon arriving at his office, Ken was glad to find Mr. Cantor's friendly face waiting for him. Ken had agreed to loosely collaborate with Mr. Cantor in deciding when to take the revised system to the next plateau. He had been looking forward to Mr. Cantor giving him the go ahead. Mr. Cantor had observed several of the first physical education classes Ken taught using the revised program. The program had been in its early stages, and there hadn't been much to see. Even then, Mr. Cantor had noticed that more students were participating in physical education class. He had told Ken that he was impressed, not only with the students' improved attitude, but also with the atmosphere of the physical education classes. He had also said that he had been glad to see students helping one another.

"Hi, Ken. The experimental unit going well?" asked Mr. Cantor as he situated himself atop Ken's desk with one foot remaining on the floor.

"Very well as a matter of fact, thanks," Ken answered proudly. "When are you coming to observe my classes again? We've made tremendous progress! You'll be amazed! The more structured curriculum and letter-grade evaluation system really motivate the students. I never expected such marked results! Once you see the results and the students' reaction to the system, there's no way anyone could question its benefits! I'm ready to take the system to the next step. What do you say?"

"Uh-huh." Mr. Cantor began to rub his chin. His eyes lit on the shoe of his dangling leg. "Ken, I can appreciate all of the effort you've put into developing and testing this new evaluation system. But I don't feel that this is the right time for the graded system. I've received some calls from parents who are . . . uh . . . uncomfortable with it. I think it would be in our best interest to put this letter-grade based evaluation system on the back burner for a while. We're not in any hurry. Let's take a step back and really look at it."

Name   Date

Questions

Preparing for Learning & Teaching

1. What is the critical issue in this case?

2. What, respectively, are Barbara Allen's and Roy King's principal perceptions of their role/job within the school?

3. How does this differ with Ken's perception of his role/job within the school?

4. How have Ken and his proposed revisions to the physical education program further stimulated a rift between him and his coworker Barbara Allen?

5. How, if in any way, do the principal's (Mr. Cantor's) interactions with Ken affect Ken's relationships with his coworkers?

6. How do you think Mr. Cantor should have reacted when pressured by parents to drop Ken's experimental units and evaluation system?

7. Taking into account Barbara Allen, Roy King, Mr. Cantor, the parents of the students, and the students themselves, are there means/methods that Ken may have overlooked but could have utilized to garner support for his new units and evaluation system?

8. After more thorough consideration of his coworkers' perspectives, should Ken revise his new evaluation proposal to create a more palatable compromise for all parties? Or should he stand his ground?

9. Rather than implementation of a new evaluation system, do you think there are other options Ken could have pursued to bring "a renewed sense of credibility" to the physical education department that would have been less drastic, more palatable, yet similarly meaningful?

10. Should Ken acquiesce and put his proposed evaluation revisions on the back burner with the hope of implementing the new system at some point in the distant future, how might he continue to maintain student accountability in his physical education classes?

11. What can Ken do should he wish to continue to pursue implementation of his new system?

12. What are some of the related issues and questions raised by this case?

13. What strategies might you use to address these issues?

Role Conflict

David Kahan

Mensah Kutame

Albert Stohrer

Case 4

J anuary 11 . . . tomorrow, winter break ends and I have to go back to school, dreading it as much as the students. We had four weeks off for the holidays and it seemed that every moment was spent either trying to make up for all the time I had spent coaching football or trying to forget about the awful football season and whether my contract would be renewed. I spent time gardening, repairing the house, playing with the baby, spent quality time with Mary, and held basketball practices. Come to think of it, the entire year repeats the holiday cycle: work, work, work, but it seems I am always doing for everyone else but me. Not that I'm complaining, but I've been teaching for only a year-and-a-half, and it already feels like five. I am racing toward burnout and saying, "Shouldn't it be easier than it is?"

Coach Eberly was revered in our town, having won five Texas small school football championships over his career; now he would help me carry on the tradition. I savored the prospect of becoming a hometown legend like Coach Eberly.

B o Rogers, a high school physical education teacher at Moraga High School in Texas, reflected on his struggle with time. He was the assistant football coach in the fall, head girls' basketball coach in the winter, and assistant track and field coach in the spring. Bo was also a member of Texas physical education and coaching associations, had been married for four years to Mary, was the father of five-month-old Kyle, and a homeowner. Bo thought back on how he had gotten to this point in his life and career, where the demands for his time far exceeded the hours in his week.

Seven years ago, I was a Moraga H.S. senior, college education secured by a full scholarship to play football at one of the state schools only 45 minutes away. I was the first in my family to go to college. Although I didn't know what I wanted to study in college, I always knew that I wanted to be involved in sports. Coach Eberly, my high school coach, called me into his office days before graduation. I had always respected Coach Eberly, and I know he liked me as well. I thought, perhaps I would like to become a coach some day—like Coach Eberly. I spoke with him about it, and he said he would help me find a place at Moraga when I graduated from college. I was honored that he thought of me in this way. Coach was revered in our town, having won five Texas small school football championships over his career; now he would help me carry on the tradition. I savored the prospect of becoming a hometown legend like Coach Eberly. On that day in his office, I decided that I would major in physical education at State, so that I could come back and coach football at Moraga.

Summer was a blur as I shuttled back and forth from home to State for weekday football practices. I was anticipating the start of school—I had been accepted into the physical education program and expected to see a lot of playing time. By October, I was on the starting line-up, and was spending more time with football and less time with my studies. I had met Mary at a fraternity party on Halloween. Surprisingly, she was a cheerleader for the football team, but I had been so consumed by football that I hadn't noticed her before. At first, we went out twice a week, but soon became inseparable. Somehow, I made C's in my classes, just avoiding academic probation. I thought I was doing okay, because as long as I graduated, a job awaited me at Moraga High. My advisor, Professor Clark, called me into his office toward the end of my sophomore year. "Bo," he said in a tone of voice that reminded me of Coach Eberly when he was disappointed, "your grades are not what they could be, and you seem to be content to coast through your classes. What do you want to make of yourself once you are finished here?"

That's an easy question, I thought, quickly replying, "I want to coach football back at Moraga when I'm through. Coach will help find a place for me."

"H'mm, I see," Professor Clark reflected, adding, "What makes you think you'll be a successful coach, or for that matter a successful teacher, if you are content to take the easy road?"

This remark sounded like something Coach Eberly used to say to challenge me, and I thought about it for the next few days. I reasoned that although I invested time and energy to be the best ball player I could be, playing ball would not last forever. I would need to grow up, make a living, and raise a family. I knew that no one just magically became good at these things. I resolved to devote myself to my studies, to be as good a teacher and coach as I was an athlete. And then there was the matter of Mary. We had been dating for close to eight months and both of us knew where our relationship was headed. We decided to get married that summer—20 years old was old enough to get married. Both of our folks were already married by the time they were our age.

During my final two years at State, Professor Clark did not call me into his office again to chastise me. On the contrary, with each passing semester Professor Clark voiced growing pleasure at my complete academic turnaround and commitment, even arranging student teaching placements so I could intern at Moraga. I had explained to him that by teaching there, I might improve my chances of landing a job after graduation, and he was very willing to help.

Coach Eberly, now in his last semester before retiring, was assigned as my mentor–teacher. I thought that it couldn't be more perfect. I would learn the ropes from a school icon; he would pass the torch to me, and I would naturally assume his job the next fall. That was the plan. But reality made me face up to some false beliefs I had held since my days as a high school student. I had been exempt from physical education as an athlete and thus had never set foot in a gym before student teaching. I was dismayed by what I saw. Each period Coach took roll for 20 minutes, rolled out a ball, and went back into his office to watch tapes of football practices. Boys played warball and girls sat and visited. There never was any trouble in his classes. Students deeply respected Coach for his football successes and resulting community pride, and were aware of what would happen if peace in the gym was disturbed. They also knew that all they had to do was show up and not bother Coach, and in return he would not "bother" them. I knew that if Professor Clark were to see this situation he would dejectedly shake his head and probably say something like, "So you want to be a football coach? What are you going to do the other 80 percent of the school day?"

My respect for Professor Clark had grown to equal the esteem I held for Coach Eberly. I had learned enough from him to know that while Coach Eberly may have been an effective coach, he was far from an effective physical education teacher. I dared not say anything to Coach about how I felt, because I didn't want to jeopardize our relationship; more importantly, I didn't want to risk losing his recommendation for a job at Moraga. I began seeing how some coaches sacrifice teaching in order to win. Maybe students don't object to a mindless, rumpus room physical education, but if one is hired to coach *and* teach, one should have the integrity to equally fulfill both responsibilities. Why didn't Coach Eberly do this? I quickly made Professor Clark aware of the situation because I knew that what I wanted to accomplish in my 10 weeks of student teaching would be unachievable due to the unstructured, throw-out-the-ball mentality of Coach Eberly. During student teaching, I learned more about what I did not want to happen in my classes than gaining any positive ideas for teaching my own students.

Two weeks after I finished student teaching, Mary and I both graduated, ready to take on the world and make our mark. We both had jobs waiting for us. A week earlier, just as I had planned, Moraga had hired me as a P. E. teacher/coach for the following fall. Mary, who had earned her degree in counseling, would assume the full-time guidance counselor position at Moraga. Amid all our good fortune, I recalled Coach Eberly's promise to take care of me, and realized that he had meant it.

The memory of that wonderful June day faded quickly as July dog days set in. We bought a fixer-upper in Moraga, and I spent almost every sweltering daylight hour sprucing it up. When I wasn't working on the house, I was at football practice. Coach Smith took over upon Coach Eberly's retirement and was determined to carry on the Moraga tradition. Coach Smith was a stocky, balding, drill-sergeant type in his late 40s and had been on Coach Eberly's staff for 17 years. The tradition in Texas sports is to reward loyalty, so it was natural for Coach Smith to succeed Coach Eberly. It suddenly dawned on me that at age 22, I was low man on the totem pole, beginning to pay my dues, conceivably for the next couple of decades, before I could be elevated to head coaching duties. It was all right though; I was living my dream, coaching football for my hometown high school.

On the schoolfront, I had four weeks before school started and no firm plans of what I wanted to do. I chanced upon a physical education curriculum guide stashed away in the department chair's office and found that the entire year was to be filled with team sports. I remembered Coach Eberly's warball games during my student teaching semester and cringed. I had learned a lot of team games at State, ones that most kids around Texas had not even heard of, let alone played—speedball, team handball, lacrosse, field hockey. I thought that by teaching these games I could entice the students with something new and different, while still adhering to the curriculum guidelines.

I was barely into the second week of school when I encountered my first official teaching problem. The students were already restless. They nagged me to play a speedball game. In Coach Eberly's units, they detoured skill development and proceeded directly into game play. "But," I said to them, "you have not yet developed the necessary skill to be successful in game play. If I let you play, it will be ragged and you won't have any fun." I had hoped that students would want to learn new skills, especially for games they had never played before. Furthermore, I thought that my new games would balance the playing field—that if none of the students had played before, then the less skilled students would feel more comfortable playing. This wasn't the case at all. Girls thought it was their right to socialize on the sidelines—it was as if these girls had been programmed by the girls from Coach Eberly's final class last spring semester. I tried modified games during the latter half of the semester with mixed results; I got more girls involved, but the boys were still unhappy. Everyday they whined, "This isn't real speedball like you explained to us. Let's play a tournament already." I guess in retrospect, the first few units and months were a breaking-in period for them and me. I inherited a P. E. program that needed as much repair work as the house Mary and I bought, and in turn the students were getting used to a teacher that would not just "roll out the ball."

I made it to winter break in one piece due in large part to the resourcefulness I had gained while at State. Professor Clark had impressed upon me the need to be accessible and not isolate myself within my gym's four walls. I had joined the Texas Association of Health, Physical Education, Recreation and Dance and the Texas High School Coaches' Association as a student and had remained active. Furthermore, I linked into these organizations and others through the Internet, thanks to the computer my parents bought me for graduation. I asked many questions and always received helpful responses. I regularly monitored the Net for any teaching tips or ideas that I could readily apply. While the teaching tips I found on the Internet didn't go over well with my students, the advice on how to respond to students' whining and complaining, offered by many experienced teachers, helped me weather through.

On the football scene, the first season had been good. Moraga advanced to the regional final, not a bad showing under a new coach. Every Saturday morning, a game story was featured on the front page of the *Moraga Bee*. I was proud to see my name in the paper and flattered to receive compliments when I was about town on errands. It soothed some of the sting I felt over the mediocrity permeating my physical education classes. I also received superior marks on my coaching evaluation. More importantly, since Coach Smith was unanimously retained, so was I. Even as a Moraga athlete, I always knew that coaches' jobs were only as secure as their win–loss percentage, but now it was me who was dependent on students' athletic success for my continued livelihood. It wouldn't matter that all my P. E. students passed their Fitnessgrams if the Moraga football team didn't make the playoffs. I breathed a sigh of relief. I'd have a job for a second year.

However, I did not rest on my laurels. Winter break may have been a break from students, but it was no break from household chores, familial obligations, or coaching. Basketball season had begun some time ago and as the new girls' basketball coach, I didn't want to let the month of conditioning prior to vacation go down the drain. I held two-hour practices four times weekly. I waited until the last minute to prepare for P. E., and then figured that I'd do better if I gave the students what they wanted—basketball, softball, and volleyball games.

Spring semester was uneventful. Physical education classes ran more smoothly from the start. I conceded that this was because I no longer held students accountable for learning and let them play games sooner. The time I saved not preparing skills and written tests for class was instead used to better prepare basketball and track practices. The girls' basketball team finished with a record that the athletic director considered acceptable, and three of my track athletes made the state meet. A small part of me was unhappy that there was little support for accomplishments outside of football. I missed the acclaim and recognition from fall football. I was excited about the prospects of a slower pace over summer vacation. However, football practices reminded me that as a teacher/coach, there is no such thing as a relaxing vacation.

A week before school started, tragedy struck. Our starting quarterback and running back were critically injured in an auto accident coming home late at night from a team party. Eyewitnesses said the car had been traveling at high speed on the wrong side of the road. Alcohol was suspected and Coach Smith came under fire for not keeping tighter control of his players. Coach proceeded to hold a team meeting, at which time he announced the immediate and indefinite suspension of four players implicated in the alcohol incident at the party. I respected his decision as morally correct, but wondered what impact it would have on the team's play.

It didn't take long to find out. Moraga started 0–2, and a couple more losses would dash any remaining hopes of a playoff appearance. The newspaper lambasted Coach Smith and his staff. Townsfolk ignored me when I was out, and publicly called for Coach Smith's head. I felt that my career was on the line. If they canned Coach Smith, my contract would almost certainly not be renewed for the following year.

I had an idea. We had two weeks to find some players who could turn the tide. I would change P. E. class so that I could use those periods as football tryouts. I would subtly suggest to the students whom I identified as prospects to speak with Coach Smith about trying out for the team. I didn't approach anyone about my idea. Coach Smith would think I was usurping his authority as head coach, while the administration, although oblivious to what went on in P. E., would frown upon such a plan. Instead, I feverishly wrote out a football unit plan and submitted it to the department head, explaining that I wanted to play football in P. E. at this time to boost school morale. Students would have fun playing football in P. E. and as a result would be more likely to come out Friday nights to cheer on the team. After all, it was a team game, and thus adhered to curriculum guidelines.

There were no problems during the first few days of the football unit. Most of the boys loved playing football any time of year. On the other hand, many of the girls were not as enthused. I learned that during Coach Eberly's football units, boys hogged games and girls never got a chance to play the key positions. I decided against forcing them to participate, knowing that it would allow me more time to evaluate the boys. Although I felt bad about indirectly excluding the girls, those not participating were content socializing on the sidelines. By Thursday I had found three possible impact players. I was going to save my job and the team. I also struggled on another level now. Two months ago our son Kyle had been born and Mary took a leave of absence, drastically reducing our income for the short term. I wanted to spend more time at home, but knew the success of the team was important if I wanted to keep my job.

During period three the following day, I ran a passing drill, where the ends run a fly, cut across the middle, and then continue running a deep pattern toward the sideline. This drill helps a coach determine receiver speed and quarterback arm strength. On the fourth play, the quarterback overthrew the receiver and struck a girl in the face as she stood on the sideline. I ran to her aid as she lay on the ground, the skin underneath her right eye badly bruised, her cheek swollen. This wasn't any injury, nor was it any girl. Sylvia was the only female student in third period with whom I didn't get along. Sylvia hated P. E. and never talked to me. And now she sported a black eye to show for P. E. class. I took her to the infirmary knowing that I was in "hot water."

If Sylvia told an administrator what had happened, I feared that I would be history. Her parents would probably sue the school and me. But I breathed a little easier when I remembered that my football unit was planned to mean nothing more than I had indicated in my unit plan, which was approved by the department head. As for any litigation that might be brought by her parents, I had forgotten that Sylvia's parents and my parents were neighbors and friends. Thank heavens for living in a small town. I was privately reprimanded by my department head and principal for running an unsafe drill. I had dodged a bullet.

I canceled the remainder of the unit, explaining to the students that I needed to have all students participating—Sylvia was hurt because she wasn't participating. I had no back-up plan for my class, because I was coming home from football practices after the 9:00 P.M. review of the game film. The students didn't buy my explanation for terminating the football unit, but they were willing to play basketball. At this point, I didn't care. I figured that I could roll out the basketballs and spend class time pouring over more game film in my office. My class climate turned decidedly colder. I heard through the grapevine that they were upset with me because Coach Eberly was predictable and I kept on changing what we did in P. E. While, externally, I rationalized my actions as a response to fears of my scheme being found out or having another student injured, internally I struggled with my conflicting beliefs. In trying to save my job and save face in the community, I had become another Coach Eberly.

The football team continued a downward slide that corresponded to events transpiring in my P. E. classes. The community would not forgive Coach Smith's 3–7 season record and seemingly my students would not forgive my error in judgment. I had worked overtime trying to salvage the season, getting home later and later with each passing week.

Mary, who had been staying at home with the baby all these months and was starved for adult company and companionship, let me know that I owed her big time come winter break. I had missed my son's first smiles and coos, disconnected from his daily life by getting home when he was already asleep and leaving before he awoke.

I've been around the house almost the entire vacation, doing things and going places together as a family, leaving only to run girls' basketball practice. I await the decision on Coach Smith's job status. I go back into the lion's den tomorrow to face the new semester's students, who undoubtedly have heard stories from last semester's students. Mary goes back to work and Kyle begins day care. This time, I don't think any advice I might find on the Internet can relieve my angst or solve my problems. I'm 24 going on 44 and wishing I was 14 again. Memories from years past flash back: of Coach Eberly praising our football team, and a touchdown I made to win a playoff game—and of Professor Clark's pride in my academic and professional development.

Name   Date

Preparing for Learning & Teaching

1. What is the critical issue in this case?

2. Can you sympathize with Bo Rogers? Give a rationale for your response.

3. In what ways does Bo's teacher education program shoulder some of the responsibility for the way things turned out?

4. What are some of the possible conflicts that can arise when one individual is both teacher and coach? How might Bo resolve the sometimes conflicting roles of teacher vs. coach?

5. How can Bo assess his priorities and gain better control of his workload?

6. What challenges can arise when we return to old settings in new roles, or work with former coaches, peers, or students in new roles?

7. What challenges arise when coaches are called upon to win games, perhaps at the cost of other programs or priorities?

8. Are there other issues beside teacher–coach role conflict, and how do they play out?

9. What strategies might you use to address the various issues?

Susan K. Lynn

Shaun M. Wuthrich

Discipline

Case 5

That's it! Joshua, where are you supposed to be?" Mr. Simmons shouted at the top of his voice. "I don't know," exclaimed Joshua with a look on his face that seemed to say that he didn't know and didn't really care. "I believe you were sent to time out until I said you could come back to activity. This is the second time I've spoken to you today," exclaimed Mr. Simmons as he moved toward Joshua. "I told you that if I had to speak to you again today I was going to write a referral." Joshua slowly shuffled his way back to the bleachers with a smug smile on his face as though the incident was a game and didn't bother him.

This was Anthony Simmons' first year at Betts Middle School. A young and energized man, Anthony had just transferred to Betts from Eudora Elementary School where he had taught physical education for five years. Unlike Eudora, Betts Middle School was an older, inner-city middle school with a low socioeconomic student population. The school was comprised of one large main building with three classroom wings surrounded by eight portable classroom buildings. All the buildings and the grounds were badly in need of repair. The physical education department had very little equipment, the gymnasium was old and had a musky smell, and the locker room walls were filled with graffiti. It was apparent to Anthony that Betts Middle School stu-

The tardy bell rang and I walked across the gym floor toward the boys' locker room. While walking I heard the muffled sound of music playing and turned my head to see Joshua Kitchens standing in the bleachers not dressed for class and dancing with a Walkman radio. Joshua was so entranced by his music and it was so loud that he had no idea I was approaching him.

dents lacked a sense of ownership and pride in their school. Betts Middle School was very different from Eudora Elementary in this respect.

Mr. Simmons watched as Joshua walked to the bleachers and sat down. Immediately he turned back to the class and tried to continue the lesson. Fortunately for Mr. Simmons, the rest of the fifth-period class generally remained on task and were very cooperative. Mr. Simmons thanked the class for their patience and cooperative behavior, then directed the students to return their ball to the bag and dress in. Mr. Simmons followed the students as they headed to the locker rooms and entered his office in the corner of the boys' locker room.

Mr. Simmons felt totally frustrated that he could not reach Joshua. It was the middle of November, over two months since the school year had begun and he still spent most of his fifth-period class trying to discipline Joshua and one of his classmates, Charise, for disruptive behavior. Joshua and Charise were both in the eighth grade and lived in the same neighborhood. While Joshua had attended Betts Middle School for three years, this was Charise's first year at the school. She had moved from another state to live with her father because her mother had remarried and Charise didn't get along very well with her stepfather. Even though Charise's father had at first resisted her mother's recommendation that Charise live with him, he had finally agreed.

After graduation from college Anthony Simmons had accepted a job teaching at Eudora Elementary because no middle or secondary positions were available at the time. Although he was certified K–12, Anthony wanted to teach at the middle-school level. This year a job opportunity opened at Betts Middle School as a result of Coach Long retiring after 30 years of teaching physical education. Having taught in the school district for five years, Anthony Simmons knew that the physical education program at Betts Middle School was known as a "busy, happy, good" program, at best. That was quite different from the program he had grown accustomed to at Eudora Elementary where developmentally appropriate activities were included and where he and his colleagues used instructional processes to meet specific goals and objectives of the program. The physical education teachers at Eudora Elementary were facilitators, and classes were student centered where the learning environment was adapted to the individual learners. Many of the learning outcomes in Eudora's physical education program were the result of not only what was being taught but how it was being taught. Nevertheless, Anthony was confident that he could improve the quality of the physical education program at Betts Middle School by helping implement, little by little, some of the same successful instructional practices that made Eudora's physical education program thrive.

The physical education faculty at Betts Middle School consisted of Anthony, Coach Graves, and a female teacher, Coach Dowlen. Both Coach Graves and Coach Dowlen had been teaching at Betts with Coach Long for 23 years. Coach Graves was the defensive line coach for the high school varsity football team and Coach Dowlen was the head softball coach at the same high school. Because of their coaching duties, Coaches

Graves and Dowlen had little energy for their physical education classes at Betts Middle School. Most of their teaching was relinquished to an organized "rolling out the ball." A new and relatively young physical education teacher such as Anthony Simmons was a big change for the physical education faculty. They had met as a faculty during one of the planning days at the beginning of school. Although they had listened to Anthony's ideas and seemed genuinely interested in what he had to say, they were not interested in making any big changes in the program. Nonetheless, Anthony felt as though he had a good social relationship with Coaches Graves and Dowlen and seemed to enjoy lunchtime chats with them.

"See ya tomorrow, Mr. Simmons!" said Todd as the bell rang for sixth period and he left the locker room. "Okay, Todd, have a good day," replied Mr. Simmons as he rubbed the sweat from his forehead. "Ahhh! My planning period," thought Mr. Simmons. As he slumped back in his chair he thought, "I guess I need to write the referral on Joshua before I do anything else. I've tried everything I know and nothing seems to work." He pulled out his student behavior log and began to reflect on all the times Joshua had disrupted class since the start of the semester, and the steps he had taken to understand why Joshua might be behaving in this manner. He didn't have to go far in the log to find his first encounter with Joshua. On page one he found his first entry. It read:

September 3, 1999. As the fifth-period class came into the gym for physical education I was standing in the doorway, monitoring students as they dispersed into respective locker rooms for dressing. I greeted several students as they entered the gymnasium. The tardy bell rang and I walked across the gym floor toward the boys' locker room. While walking I heard the muffled sound of music playing and turned my head to see Joshua Kitchens standing in the bleachers not dressed for class and dancing with a Walkman radio. Joshua was so entranced by his music and it was so loud that he had no idea I was approaching him. Gently, I turned the Walkman off. I reminded him that one of the school rules was that students were not to have Walkmans at school. I told him that if he would give the radio to me I would lock it in my desk drawer until the end of the school day. Joshua refused and said that he would put it in his P. E. locker. I told Joshua that I would have to confiscate the radio until after school. I told him he could give me the radio now and I would give it back to him after school, or I would report it to the office and call his parents. Joshua ripped the headphones from his ears and slapped the radio into my hands. I told him to get dressed for class, but he refused and took a seat on the bleachers. I talked with him after class about his behavior; however, he really didn't seem to care.

September 6, 1999. I spoke with Joshua about not dressing out for class all week. Joshua told me that he hated soccer. I told him that his failure to dress out and participate would have an adverse effect on his grade. I told him that I thought he would be a good soccer player if he would only give it a try. Joshua's reply was that he would think about it.

September 10, 1999. What a day! I put Joshua and Charise in time out for fighting over a soccer ball. This happened to be the very same day and class period that Mr. O'Donnell, the vice-principal, stopped by my class on his way to the parking lot. While I was demonstrating heading a soccer ball, I noticed that most eyes were not on me but on something or someone behind me. I stopped demonstrating, turned around, and looked. To my surprise I saw Mr. O'Donnell standing under a tree and looking up. At first, I thought he was carrying on a conversation with the tree, but then to my horror I saw Charise and Joshua shimmy down out of the tree! After school I tried to call both students' parents but got no answer. I left a message on their answering machines to please call me at home tonight.

September 13, 1999. Didn't get a call last night from Joshua's or Charise's parents. I reached Joshua's mother at work this morning but never got in touch with Charise's father. Joshua's mother said she was sorry that he had been disrespectful and that she would talk to him. She explained that she and his father had recently divorced and that she was having a tough time with Joshua at home. She said he just didn't seem to care about anything. I asked her if she thought he might need some counseling. She said absolutely, but that money was tight and her insurance would not cover counseling services.

September 14, 1999. Spoke with the guidance counselor about my concerns regarding Joshua's behavior at school and at home. She told me to send him to her office when he came to physical education. I sent Joshua to guidance at the beginning of class.

September 15, 1999. Spoke with Joshua twice during the lesson for kicking another group's soccer ball across the field. Removed him from the lesson on the third time and spoke with him after class.

September 20, 1999. This is the fourth day Joshua has not dressed out for class. On the way in from the soccer field a verbal confrontation occurred between Charise and Joshua. I stepped in just as Charise was getting ready to hit Joshua with her fist. Charise was teasing Joshua about his worn tennis shoes to which Joshua replied that Charise only wished her feet were small enough to wear his shoes. I told them that if they could not say anything kind to keep their mouths closed and keep those thoughts to themselves.

September 27, 1999. I had to sit Joshua out in class today for kicking other students in the shin while trying to steal the soccer ball. I praised him for working hard but told him he was just playing too rough. After the second warning I had to sit him out. He got very mad, left the field, and walked to the gym. I tried to talk to Joshua when I brought the class in but he refused to talk to me.

September 30, 1999. Joshua has not dressed out since September 27th. Met with several of his teachers to discuss the problems I was having with him. The other teachers reported that many of the same behaviors were happening in their classrooms. We decided that each of us should do a contingency plan for our class with Joshua. I felt much better after leaving the meeting. I knew we could help Joshua if we all worked together.

October 1, 1999. Called Joshua's mother and told her about the meeting and our decision to each write a contingency plan with Joshua. She was grateful.

October 4, 1999. Met with Joshua during my planning period to discuss making a contingency plan. We talked about his failure to dress out and participate in class activities and his inability to work quietly and cooperatively when he did join the class. I asked him to write down three behaviors that he felt he could improve. We discussed his goals and came to an agreement. Progress at last.

Students, may I have your attention please." Mr. Simmons jumped as the afternoon announcements blasted through the intercom speaker in his office. "Those students who ride Bus 43, Ms. Jackson's bus, will be riding Bus 15, Mr. Perry's bus today. I repeat, those students who ride Bus 43, Ms. Jackson's bus, will be riding Bus 15, Mr. Perry's bus today. Thank you."

He was only through the first month of notes. He had another month and a half to go with probably some 20 or more entries in his log. Reading the log only reminded him of how excited and hopeful he had been earlier in the semester about helping Joshua work through this difficult period in his life. Unfortunately, nothing that he had done had helped improve Joshua's behavior in his class. He had spoken to the guidance counselor and Joshua's mom repeatedly, but every effort they made failed to reach Joshua. He had probably stayed after school with Joshua more in the past two months than he had in his entire five years at Eudora Elementary. He was sad and frustrated that all his efforts had resulted in this referral.

Mr. Simmons put his final comments on the referral just as the bell rang to end the day. After serving his duty monitoring the hallway outside the gymnasium, he made his way to the office. As Mr. Simmons was placing the referral in Mr. O'Donnell's box he heard, "How's it going, Anthony?" It was Mr. O'Donnell coming to check the mail in his box. "Actually I've been having some discipline problems with a couple of students and one student in particular, Joshua Kitchens. I was just leaving this referral for you," replied Mr. Simmons as he handed the document to Mr. O'Donnell. As he took the referral Mr. O'Donnell laughed and said, "Oh yes, one of the tree climbers from your fifth-period class. Well, if you have a few minutes we can go into my office and talk about it." Mr. Simmons accepted the invitation and followed Mr. O'Donnell down the short hallway into his office.

Mr. O'Donnell began the conversation as he pulled open a file cabinet drawer and took out a file on Joshua Kitchens. As he sat down at his desk he said, "Well, I see from your referral that you have taken a number of steps to handle Mr. Kitchens yourself. Let's see, you say that you've warned him and removed him from the class, talked with him repeatedly after class, separated him from Charise, spoke with his other teachers, called his parents, and tried a contingency contract." Mr. O'Donnell looked up from his desk and said, "It looks as though you've taken appropriate steps, Anthony. I certainly wish all our teachers would go the lengths that you have. You've done far more than I would have done with that kid. I will call Joshua in tomorrow and give him three days of after-school detention, OK?" "But Mr. O'Donnell," exclaimed Mr. Simmons as he moved to the edge of his chair, "he's had after-school detention a thousand times and it has no effect on the kid!" "Well, Anthony," said Mr. O'Donnell calmly, "what would you suggest I do?" Mr. Simmons quickly replied, "He needs to be taken out of the class when he misbehaves. At that point, I would like to send Joshua straight to the office. He is totally disruptive and preventing the rest of the class from learning. These other students in the class have a right to learn!" Mr. O'Donnell's voice raised as he told Anthony, "You know you're not the only faculty having discipline problems with Joshua Kitchens; however, you are the only physical education teacher that has ever had a problem. Maybe you should talk to Coach Graves and Coach Dowlen. And besides, Joshua can't spend the whole day in the office! I will speak with him, but he's not going to sit in the front office during physical education because that's depriving Joshua of an education. I trust you can and will handle the situation." "That's it?" Mr. Simmons asked as he moved back in his seat. "I'm afraid that's all we can do for now. Now, if you will excuse me, Anthony, I have a meeting to attend," replied Mr. O'Donnell as he exited his office.

Mr. Simmons slowly lifted himself out of the chair and walked out of the office. His frustration was bordering on anger as he walked back to his office. "This is absolutely ridiculous; how many times does it take or how many teachers have to report this kid for the administration to take some real action?" Anthony thought. "I've done everything I can do to correct the problem in the classroom without asking the administration for help. Now that I have asked for help, they are not willing to take a next step." As Anthony approached his office door he stopped, looked around, and thought, "Why did I ever leave Eudora Elementary? I must have been crazy to come here. Doesn't Mr. O'Donnell realize that we're not helping Joshua by sending him to after-school detention for the millionth time!"

In a flash he unlocked the door, grabbed his briefcase, lunch box, and gym bag, and headed for the parking lot. It was raining hard but he didn't want to wait; he needed to get to the gym as quickly as possible. A long, hard workout would certainly improve his state of mind. Maybe then he could figure out what to do. About a mile from the school he passed Joshua walking along the side of the road in the driving rain. He knew where Joshua lived, which meant he had several more miles to go, so he slowed down and pulled over. "Joshua," Mr. Simmons yelled, "would you like a lift home?" "Thank you, Mr. Simmons, I sure would!" cried Joshua as he ran to the car, drenched from head to toe. It was at that moment that Mr. Simmons knew why he had left Eudora Elementary; it was for Joshua Kitchens.

Name   Date

Preparing for Learning & Teaching

1. What is the critical issue in this case?

2. In this case, Mr. Simmons called Joshua's and Charise's parents. If you were responsible for calling the parents to inform them of the circumstances, what would you do?

3. Mr. Simmons and the vice-principal seem to be at odds with one another. What kinds of things can a physical education teacher do to increase the likelihood of support from a vice-principal if and when a difficult situation arises?

4. The teachers in this case decided to create a behavior-management contingency plan for Joshua. Discuss this method.

5. Is it the job of the school to discipline the student who is not receiving proper guidance at home? Why or why not?

6. Is it the job of the school to provide counseling for a student who is having emotional difficulties but is not able to afford out-of-school professional counseling? Why or why not?

7. At what point, if any, should a child be removed from the classroom? Who should make this decision?

8. What are the related issues and questions raised by this case?

9. What role did the characters play in creating/solving these issues?

10. What are some of the suggested strategies you might use to address these issues?

Emyr W. Williams

Gary D. Kinchin

Inclusion I

Case 6

Mary took the last three steps of the gym stairway in one bound. As she entered the physical education office, an excited young voice bellowed from behind, "Have a great holiday, Miss Wong." Mary turned and saw Tom, a grinning eighth-grade student with book-bag bulging over his shoulder. She waved at Tom and replied, "Good luck with your basketball tournament. With all the scheduled games, you should be in great shape for the New Year." Mary picked up the pile of Christmas cards she'd received from the students. The top one read, "Have a great vacation. Thanks for all the help this semester." All of the seventh-grade students in fifth period had signed their names on the card. Mary knew now that the holiday season was about to begin. She'd survived her first semester of teaching middle school physical education.

Mary left college with an excellent report following her student teaching experience at an urban middle school. She had received her undergraduate degree and teaching certification from a large Midwestern university. Following graduation Mary decided to forego seeking teaching positions in the large city in which she'd trained, instead choosing to return to her suburban home-town to teach. Teaching had been her life-long ambition. Both her parents were teachers and they had encouraged her to pursue this career. Mary accepted a position at Range Hill Middle School in northwestern Ohio. Range Hill

"Miss Wong?" a voice inquired, "I'm John Conner, Sally's dad. I want to know why you have not been helping my daughter in her physical education classes. I have a copy of her IEP here with me, and would like to go over this with you now!"

Middle School had a student population of 550. Located in a fairly afflu-ent middle-class suburban area, students were mostly white (95 percent), with the other 5 percent predominantly African American. During the interview Mary had been impressed by the innovative and progressive philosophy of the school, and the teachers' dedication to student learn-ing. She was delighted when they offered her the position. Mary antici-pated that working at an idyllic school like Range Hill would enable her to attain many professional attributes characteristic of an effective teacher.

Although the holiday season was upon her, Mary was feeling physi-cally and mentally drained. As the hallway door slammed, a wry smile came over her face. Mary said to herself, "That Tom, he's not stopped beaming from the first day of class." Tom's toothy grin would be a mem-ory to cherish over the holidays.

Rocking back on her chair, Mary's smile quickly faded as her eyes focused upon the large manila folder on the shelf above her file cabinet. Sally Conner's bulging file was a reminder of one of the few bothersome aspects of her first semester at Range Hill. Mary's mind wandered back to the new teacher orientation meeting before the start of the semester with the principal, Ms. Webb. In that meeting the new teachers were informed about the inclusion policy of the district. There were 11 stu-dents with Severe Behavior Handicaps (SBH) attending Range Hill. At the end of the meeting, Principal Webb asked Mary to stay behind. Ms. Webb informed Mary that as she was new to the physical education department, she wasn't going to be required to accept any students with SBH in her classes this academic year, although she would definitely have students with SBH in her classes next year. However, this year, if Mary didn't wish to take any students with SBH, they would be includ-ed in Mr. Brady's physical education classes. Ms. Webb added that it might be beneficial for Mary to work with a child with diverse behavior, such as Sally Conner, as it would give her valuable experience. At the same time, it would reduce the number of students with SBH that Mr. Brady (the only other physical educator at the school) would have. Rising quickly from behind her desk, Ms. Webb picked up her briefcase and headed toward the door. While opening the door for Mary, Ms. Webb stated, "I have every confidence that you'd do a great job with Sally. I must go—more meetings at district headquarters. It's going to be anoth-er long night. If you have a problem with including Sally in your class this year, make an appointment with my secretary to discuss this further. But, I believe you'll do fine." Ms. Webb left Mary to deliberate on what she'd been volunteered for.

Sally Conner had just been moved up to the seventh grade. Sally was prescribed Ritalin (a drug commonly used to treat hyperactive children). Her father had recently taken a job, after being unemployed for over a year. His new position involved extensive traveling and very little time at home. An assessment by the district psychologist indicated that Sally felt deserted by her father's absence from home, and unfairly treated by her mother. Sally stated that her mother always blamed her, instead of her two younger brothers, when any disputes arose within the family.

Sally's attendance at school was inconsistent. Her mother had a difficult time getting Sally to school some days, due to her indifference. Occasionally she had to walk her to first period and remain there until the teacher arrived. This was the extent of Mrs. Conner's contact with Sally's teachers. A number of attempts by the school to arrange parent–teacher conferences were thwarted by Mrs. Conner. With her husband away nearly all of the time, and having to look after the two young boys, Mrs. Conner said that she didn't have time to attend parent–teacher conferences concerning Sally's behavior in school.

Mary recalled the first physical education unit of the year—soccer. Those balmy September days seemed an age ago. Mary could tell that Sally wasn't excited by soccer simply by her body language. Sally was shy and intimidated by the other students. The first few lessons were fine because she worked alone. As the unit progressed, she refused to participate in group activities. Mary recalled the fifth day of the unit when Sally sat on the field and refused to budge. Mary took time out from the rest of the class in an attempt to encourage Sally to play. After nearly five minutes Sally agreed to join in on one condition: Mary had to be her partner. Mary agreed, while the rest of the class continued to work with minimal guidance from the teacher. At the lesson's end, Mary placed her hand on Sally's shoulder and praised her for the good work during that lesson. Mary and Sally's partnership became the pattern for the next two lessons.

By the end of the second week, Sally's expectation to always pair up with Mary had become unacceptable for Mary. Feeling that she couldn't devote all of her time to Sally, while the other students were essentially fending for themselves, Mary decided to stop being Sally's partner. For the next two days Sally refused to participate in any way. Mary, in return, avoided devoting any time to Sally. Sally's classmates tried to encourage her to join in but they also became tired of her behavior. Finally, Mary sat down with Sally in the office to talk to her about her unacceptable behavior, the help others were trying to give her, and her refusal to accept it. All Sally could say was, "No one likes me. My mom doesn't like me, my dad always leaves me, those kids always tease me, and you won't help me." Mary said that Sally must learn to join in, that there were 27 other children in the class that needed help too; she wasn't the only one. Sally erupted into a major tantrum and stormed out. Mary shouted for her to come back, but Sally disappeared into the hive of activity in the corridor.

Timmy and Jane, from Sally's soccer class, came to Mary upset because some of the students in their group were goofing off. Mary couldn't see this because she had been spending so much time with Sally. The two students also told her that the bigger kids were dominating the play every lesson, and they didn't think it was fair. "We both like soccer and want to learn about the game and improve our skills," Timmy and Jane complained. Mary had apologized and promised that things would be different, that she would spend more time with all of the students.

Mary reflected on the tough lesson that she'd experienced and considered strategies she could introduce to rectify the situation. Mary recalled her first conversation with Range Hill's SBH specialist, Gordon Bennett, after he had observed Sally in Mary's class. Mr. Bennett was responsible for the welfare of the 11 students with SBH attending Range Hill. Gordon admitted that he had trouble working with Sally and in establishing lines of communication with her parents. He suggested that Mary document Sally's behavior and contact him if necessary. At that time Mary did not realize how much material she would be gathering about Sally.

Initially Mary jotted brief notes on Sally's inappropriate behavior, however, as the semester progressed, these notes lengthened, becoming more detailed. Frequently Mary had one-on-one conversations with Sally at the end of the lesson, and the topics of these encounters were kept on file. Concurrently dated records of Mary's attempts to contact Sally's parents, as well as the conversations she had with Mrs. Conner, were recorded with the notes supplied on weekly contacts with Mr. Bennett. Additionally, other students' complaints concerning Sally's behavior in class were noted. Finally, Sally's attendance record was included in the file.

Although Mary kept in contact with Gordon Bennett throughout the semester, she had reservations about seeking administrative support. After all, she had agreed to have Sally in her class. Additionally she felt that a cry for help would present an unfavorable impression of her teaching competence in the eyes of the administrators.

The second unit of the year had been gymnastics. Mary shook her head as she remembered the ordeal of those lessons. Sally again demanded Mary's undivided time and attention. Julia, another member of the class, had kindly offered to help Sally and be her spotter. Sally, however, refused to have anything to do with Julia or any of the other students. Occasionally, at the end of some class periods, Sally would start to participate and Mary would encourage her. Initially, Mary even forfeited some of her lunch break to talk with Sally in the hope that her behavior would change for the better. This pattern of only starting to work at the end of the lesson continued until Mary realized that this was Sally's way of monopolizing her attention. The next lesson Sally spent the first 40 minutes of a 45-minute lesson in the bleachers. Five minutes before class finished, Sally got up and was ready to begin. Mary said that this would have to stop as she had other obligations to attend to during her lunch hour. Sally burst into tears and left the gymnasium. For the past week or so, Sally has refused to dress and participate in any of her physical education classes.

As Mary began to gather her things, she wondered if Sally would be back after the holiday break. Just as Mary was about to switch off the office lights there was a knock at the door. "Miss Wong?" a voice inquired, "I'm John Conner, Sally's dad. I want to know why you have not been helping my daughter in her physical education classes. I have a copy of her IEP [Individualized Education Program] here with me, and would like to go over this with you now!"

Acknowledgment

The authors wish to thank Jane Mabry, Becky Grimes, and Barry Lavay for their input on this case.

Name   Date

Preparing for Learning & Teaching

1. What is the primary issue within this case?

2. What circumstances contributed to the issue?

3. At what point within the case could there have been intervention(s)? What personnel might have/should have initiated this intervention? What could they have done to address the issue?

4. What might have been some consequences of the(se) intervention(s) for the student (Sally), the teacher (Mary), or the school?

5. What role did the major characters play in creating the issue within the case?

6. How do you think Mary might handle the conversation with John Conner?

7. What impact might the IEP have on the dialogue between John and Mary?

8. What could Mary have said to the principal (Ms. Webb) at the initial meeting?

9. What factors might have impacted Mary's decision to refuse Sally's inclusion into the class?

10. What further instructional strategies could Mary have adopted in the soccer and gymnastics units to better include Sally?

11. What are the related issues and questions raised by this case?

12. What are some of the strategies you might use to address these issues?

Resistance to Change

Lynn Schincariol

Ann-Catherine Sullivan

Roberta Faust

Tracy Wright

Case 7

Jumping into her Jeep following her final interview, Coty was reflecting on the prospects of an exciting new career. Finally, a chance with her own students, her own program, and her own curriculum. During the interview process she had outlined her teaching philosophy and her desire to implement a fitness-based curriculum for middle school students, which she had been developing over the past year. Coty smiled as she recalled the enthusiasm and support the principal displayed for her fitness curriculum ideas. His words and actions led her to believe that he was in favor of implementing her curriculum into his school and that he would support her throughout the implementation process.

Coty had taken an indirect route to obtain her teaching certification. Her undergraduate degree was in textiles and design, a field she had worked in for seven years. Coty had been an active person her whole life and remained active during that time. Eventually, her passion for working out led her to acquire the necessary qualifications to earn her American College of Sports Medicine (ACSM) personal trainer certification. Through her work in the health and fitness industry,

Standing on the sidelines, Coty shuddered as she watched her mentor teach the first few classes of the year. Her heart sank as she watched students completing exercises on command. "Up Down Up Down," he demanded through the still air of the gymnasium. His commanding style went against everything she believed.

she began to realize how little people actually knew about fitness. She decided that one way to overcome this was to go back to school to become a physical education teacher. She reasoned that as a teacher, she

53

would be able to educate students in the basics of fitness, and in doing so, arm them with the knowledge and skills that would enable them to live active, healthy lifestyles.

Coty enrolled in a one-year master of education teacher certification program. Her master's coursework required her to complete a research project. Aware that there was no fitness component in the local public middle school curriculum, Coty was spurred on to develop a fitness curriculum for this group of learners. She diligently worked on her curriculum research project from her entrance into the program in September through August graduation.

Coty was thrilled to receive her secondary student teaching placement at a local middle school. Finally, an opportunity to pilot her innovative curriculum. Coty met with her cooperating teacher and discussed the possibility of developing and teaching a fitness unit to the seventh- and eighth-grade students. Although fitness was not a scheduled unit, the cooperating teacher agreed to let Coty teach the unit. As was her nature, Coty assiduously began working on her plan. She had several meetings with her university advisor and supervisor, at which she requested feedback on her unit and lesson plans. Several revisions later, she had a completed plan and was anxious, eager, and excited about implementing its content.

Her secondary placement was at an International Middle School where the student population represented a variety of different social and cultural backgrounds from various countries. At the time, the two full-time physical education teachers utilized a traditional sport skill curriculum model. The male physical educator resembled a textbook description of a "roll-out-the-ball" teacher. He never once talked to the students; rather, he barked at them. The other teacher, a female, was Coty's cooperating teacher. She was known by the university to be an effective and caring teacher. During the time Coty was assigned to work with her, she was attending the local university part-time in an effort to complete her master's degree.

Coty's cooperating teacher wanted Coty to organize and teach a physical education program where the students learned the skills and tactics of the game, and learned how to play together and respect one another. However, her colleague, who had been there for several years prior to her arrival and who ran the program, would have nothing to do with such a program. He was close to retirement and was very content to "just let 'em play." To compromise, Coty's cooperating teacher agreed to be responsible for the teaching and her teaching partner agreed to be responsible for the discipline. However, when Coty was actually implementing her units, the cooperating teacher and university supervisor spoke to the male physical educator and asked him to let Coty take control of the class. He agreed.

During the days leading up to Coty's fitness unit, she presented her first few lesson plans to her cooperating teacher, and together they discussed and refined the content, transitions, student groupings, and activities. Finally, the day had come. Coty arrived at the school excited and eager to begin her unit. As she began her first lesson, she outlined the expectations for the students during the upcoming weeks. Coty received a few grumblings, but not many. However, when she actually began teaching the content and the students realized she actually expected them to do some work, the students challenged and opposed her efforts. Initially she was disappointed but remained optimistic. She rationalized to herself and verbalized to her cooperating teacher and university supervisor that it would just take some time—time to get used to her and her expectations. She persisted. After each lesson she would engage her cooperating teacher in conversation in an effort to search for ways to reach her students. No matter what she tried, the students continued to resist and oppose her efforts. As the unit progressed, Coty became more and more frustrated. The students were not accustomed to anything but "playing the game" in gym class, and they were not going to change for her. Coty kept telling herself it would be better when she had her own classes and she was able to organize and manage her own program.

When Coty accepted her first teaching position, she thought it would be a dream come true, but her idealistic vision of implementing her fitness curriculum was clouded minutes after meeting her new teaching colleague and assigned mentor. Her teaching partner, who also considered himself the department head, handed her the assigned teaching units for the year. Breathing a sigh of exasperation, Coty could not believe what lay in front of her. She was looking at four basketball units, two track and field units, and one dance unit. Coty's dream was shattered.

This was her first teaching position, a rural middle school located just outside of a large metropolitan area. It should have been the ideal setting for implementing her fitness curriculum—not only did the school service sixth-, seventh-, and eighth-grade students, but the students received physical education five days per week. "This was the situation I had in mind when I designed my fitness curriculum," she thought to herself.

For the past year and a half Coty had been led to believe that when she got her own classes she would be able to set up and teach her own curriculum. She was having second thoughts about accepting a position where the curriculum was already established and her colleague's teaching style and philosophy could not have been more diametrical to her own. What should she do? What could she do?

In an effort to gain an appreciation for her teaching colleague's style and grasp a better understanding of the expectations of the administration, she agreed to team-teach the first couple of lessons with her new peer. Since he insisted on initially taking control, Coty reluctantly agreed to let him take over the first day.

Standing on the sidelines, she shuddered as she watched her mentor teach the first few classes of the year. Her heart sank as she watched students completing exercises on command. "Up Down Up Down," he demanded through the still air of the gymnasium. She watched in disbelief as the students performed pushups, their bodies rising and falling in response to the commands of the bellowing voice. His commanding style went against everything she believed. Coty knew she could not teach this way. She instantly realized it would be difficult to teach her classes simultaneously on the other side of the gymnasium while he continuously shouted commands at his students.

Coty returned to her office to contemplate the next step. Her mind was racing, "Can I do this, how can I do this, will I be able to teach my curriculum, how am I going to talk over his bellowing voice, where does fitness fit into this environment?" Her head dropped in her hands for a moment, then Coty tried to focus on the days ahead. She thought to herself, "I'm not gonna give up. I've worked too hard for this. I believe in this too strongly. How can I do this? How can I do this?" she whispered to herself. After some thought, "That's it," she exclaimed, jumping up from her chair.

During week one, as Coty outlined and demonstrated her rules and routines, she informed the students that they were expected to engage in and complete various activities aimed at improving their fitness. Each lesson's warm-up began by focusing on various components of fitness. The students were told they would be working in teams. Within their teams, each member would complete a cardiovascular warm-up, activity-specific stretching daily, and muscular endurance exercises twice weekly. Similar to establishing other rules and routines, Coty had to continuously encourage and reinforce her students' compliance with this routine.

By January, Coty sensed that she had made some progress with the administration and her teaching peer toward building a solid case for her fitness curriculum. She had succeeded in infusing fitness into all her units. During her third unit of basketball, Coty stood back and observed how her students independently carried out their warm-up routines. A feeling of satisfaction overcame her as she watched her students automatically gather into their established teams and begin to complete the cardiovascular component of the warm-up, and then move into their activity-specific stretches. Following this, they all checked the board to see if any muscular endurance activities were required, then regrouped as a team to continue with their warm-up or to wait for Coty's next instruction. Coty was free to circulate and interact with her students, chat about outside interests, and provide positive feedback. She reflected back over the months of struggle that led her to this point. "It's not perfect," she thought, "but at least it's a start."

Coty continued to believe that things would only get better. She became excited again, when the principal asked her for a copy of her fitness curriculum. She still believed that she had administrative support to implement her ideas.

During the summer Coty scoured numerous fitness resources looking for programs and activities that would align with her current teaching context and the needs of her students. Finding a program she believed was better suited for her students, she began to refine and rewrite her lessons. Her eyes lit up and a huge smile crossed her face as she discussed her work with graduate students over the summer. As the summer came to an end, she was excited about beginning her second year.

Walking into her office the week before classes were to start, Coty was shocked to see a lone white sheet of paper resting on her desk with the title "1998–99 Teaching Schedule: Physical Education" in big, bold, black letters across the top. Surprise, surprise—fitness was not even mentioned on the assigned schedule.

Questions
Preparing for Learning & Teaching

1. What is the critical issue in this case?

2. How can Coty make it through another year without compromising her values? How would you make this situation work for you?

3. What support systems seem to be working for Coty? Where else could Coty obtain support?

4. What steps could Coty take in renegotiating with the principal and her teaching colleague to assure inclusion of her fitness curriculum for the next school year?

5. What strategies could Coty use to keep herself motivated in a positive direction during this difficult time?

6. What are the related issues and questions raised by this case?

7. What are the strategies you might use to address these issues?

Toward Collaboration

Monica Lounsbery
Marian Nielsen
Tom Sharpe
Sheba Stevens

Case

8

Dr. Jan Watson

Shaking her head in disbelief, Dr. Watson felt a surge of anger and frustration sweep over her as she made her way to leave a university-wide secondary teacher education advisory board meeting. As a first year assistant professor, Dr. Watson had been invited to participate on the university-wide board. The board had just adopted a new clinical experience requirement in secondary teacher preparation. It was not the new requirement that elicited such negative feelings from Dr. Watson, as she believed strongly in the importance of practical teaching experiences prior to student teaching. It was her passionate disagreement with the advisory board's recommendation concerning how clinical experiences would be implemented and evaluated that brought on her anger; especially since the university had a large teacher education component and was already inundating the public schools with preservice teachers. Typical of many postsecondary advisory board practices, this board had voted that each methods course instructor at the university would be required to place students into a public school clinical experience. This, of course, was without any forethought regarding who would structure the experience, provide feedback and goal-setting information, or evaluate the experience in any ongoing way. Therefore, what would more than likely happen would

Dr. Watson's thoughts turned back to the university advisory board meeting and her feelings of frustration. "It's as if these people have never truly 'worked' with anyone, let alone public school teachers," she thought to herself.

59

be that all of these responsibilities would be dumped on to the public school teachers with whom clinical experience students are placed.

While it is true that the university cannot provide preservice teachers with contextually accurate teaching experiences without the help of public school faculty, the responsibility for structuring those experiences, providing ongoing instruction and mentorship, and evaluation should clearly be a shared responsibility between university and school-based personnel. Dr. Watson argued her viewpoints intensely to the board, only to be indirectly dismissed as being, "that new faculty member from physical education," a department clearly viewed by the board to be of marginal importance to the teacher education mission of the university.

Dr. Watson was beginning the third quarter of her first academic year as an assistant professor within a comprehensive Research I university. Prior to accepting this position, Dr. Watson had finished her graduate work at another institution, where her primary role was to direct and coordinate the university/school partnership activities within an established physical education teacher education program. During her graduate studies, Dr. Watson directed the ongoing activities of multiple professional development schools (PDS), taught as a demonstration teacher within these schools, provided ongoing evaluations of undergraduate students as they matriculated through their clinical experiences in these sites, and conducted applied research in these sites in collaboration with her faculty mentors and other graduate students.

During the course of Dr. Watson's PDS and related graduate studies involvement, she grew committed to the value of clinical experiences for teachers-in-training and could see the difference in those who were involved in these experiences versus those who were not. As a function of these experiences, Dr. Watson also learned first hand of the many inherent challenges to forging positive working relationships with a variety of public school personnel. She thought about how beneficial it had been for all participants when she would sit down with undergraduates and practicing teachers after a practice teaching episode and discuss as equal contributing partners the many effective, and sometimes not-so-effective, portions of a particular lesson activity. All would provide input, and all would benefit greatly from listening to the perspective of the others, Dr. Watson included. Teachers would often comment on how "rejuvenating" it was to observe and participate in the educational process of prospective teachers. Undergraduates began to genuinely listen to and implement the combined recommendations for improved teaching. University personnel benefited from an increased awareness of the challenges of contemporary public school practice and began to think in terms of more relevant and meaningful applied research activities.

Dr. Watson also spent many hours talking informally with the PDS teachers to elicit their ideas about ways to improve the preparation of future teachers. She was no longer surprised when she heard the most frequently voiced complaint: when the university sends students out to the public schools, a university representative typically is not present. Many remarked that the traditional custodial model of teacher preparation, in which universities use the public schools as "dumping grounds" for their students, was simply not working and was very frustrating on the part of the public schools. Such an approach was viewed by most as only contributing to the widening gap between university-based teacher education programs and the world of public school teaching practice. In addition, such a tradition caused school-based personnel to view with great skepticism any university faculty seeking to establish a partnership activity.

Dr. Watson's thoughts turned back to the university advisory board meeting and her feelings of frustration. "It's as if these people have never truly 'worked' with anyone, let alone public school teachers," she thought to herself. To truly "work" with others, one must at least be present, fumed Dr. Watson. In addition to being present, Dr. Watson wanted to make the point that ongoing communication is a critical element, and the ability to continually listen and encourage input from teachers is of utmost importance if a partnership is going to thrive. She sighed deeply as she arrived at her office door. As Dr. Watson entered and slumped into her chair, she concluded that despite her frustrations there existed hope for a model partnership to be forged in physical education teacher education. She resolved to roll up her sleeves and get such a program started according to how she thought it should be accomplished. She glanced down at her unopened mail and found four of the return envelopes that she had included in a partnership correspondence to area physical education teachers. "I actually got some responses already," she thought to herself and with renewed effort forged ahead on her own.

A few days prior to the university advisory board meeting, Dr. Watson had written a letter introducing herself as a new physical education faculty member to all of the secondary physical education teachers in the area. The letter explained that she was very interested in collaborating with local schoolteachers and principals and would call to set up a personal visit with all those who were interested in beginning some form of partnership activity. Sensitive to the tight time schedules of most public school personnel, Dr. Watson took great care to ensure there would be little burden involved in expressing potential interest. In the correspondence she enclosed a self-addressed stamped envelope, and in the letter a teacher who wished to respond could simply check a box and indicate various levels of interest.

Dr. Watson opened the envelopes before her and found that all of the responses were from teachers working in Johnson Middle School. The responses, while not openly enthusiastic, indicated some interest in establishing a partnership. "Hmm, I bet these teachers worked with Dr. Mann prior to his departure," she thought to herself. Dr. Mann had recently left the university to take an administrative position at a smaller college. Dr. Mann had accomplished a great deal during his tenure at this university and was a very well-respected faculty member among his colleagues. He had also experienced some success in placing his teacher candidates locally over the years, providing a positive connection with the surrounding public school system. Dr. Watson had been hired to replace Dr. Mann, and from listening to her new colleagues talk about

Dr. Mann's accomplishments, she knew that while filling his shoes may provide challenges at times, Dr. Mann's prior efforts would also facilitate what she wanted to accomplish professionally.

The next day Dr. Watson telephoned Johnson Middle School and asked to speak to the physical education department. Her call was routed to one of the teachers who had responded. Dr. Watson introduced herself, and stated her business very quickly, knowing that this teacher was likely between classes and busy with more immediate tasks. Through the conversation, Dr. Watson learned that the physical education department at Johnson Middle School was very unified and committed to a skill-based physical education program. In addition, as past colleagues of Dr. Mann, the teachers were receptive and enthusiastic about an initial meeting to discuss the possibility of working with the university program in various capacities. The phone conversation ended when the teacher stated that a Ms. Smithers was the department head for their physical education program and that all meeting times and related decisions would need to be cleared through her. Dr. Watson asked the teacher to take down her phone number and to leave a message to have Ms. Smithers call her when she had a free moment.

As Dr. Watson hung up the phone, she was not as optimistic about the potential of placing university clinical experience students at this middle school. From the tone of the conversation, she sensed that there was some reluctance, and wondered about the cause of the hesitancy. She went next door to the office of one of her colleagues to ask him about some of the history of Dr. Mann's clinical experiences. He pulled out a formatted letter and explained that Dr. Mann would send the letter out to all area secondary physical education teachers and that the letter asked teachers to respond if they were interested in mentoring a clinical experience for a particular student. All teachers who responded with interest were then placed on a list. The list was then distributed to students in the class, and from the list Dr. Mann would have students self-select into a clinical experience and make all introductions.

"And that worked?" Dr. Watson exclaimed with surprise. "Oh yeah," her colleague responded. "We've never had a problem. We've been doing this long before the advisory board voted to require clinical experiences," he added. Dr. Watson inquired whether these experiences were ever supervised by anyone from the university and was told no, but that Dr. Mann worked with the teachers on several research publication projects and frequented the school often. Finally, she asked about the teachers at Johnson Middle School. She was told that all six teachers on staff had previously worked with Dr. Mann. She thanked her colleague and returned to her office to find the phone ringing.

When she answered, Sally Smithers, the physical education program director at Johnson Middle School, was on the line. Dr. Watson agreed to meet Ms. Smithers in her office before school the next day. When she arrived the next morning one of the teachers, Mrs. Snow, was waiting at the door. She welcomed Dr. Watson to Johnson Middle School and introduced herself. Dr. Watson was impressed by Mrs. Snow's professionalism.

After showing Dr. Watson the school facilities, Mrs. Snow led her to the girl's locker room, where the office space was shared by some of the other physical education specialists. When they entered the office, Sally Smithers was seated at her desk and four other physical educators were also present.

Once introduced, and after some small talk, Dr. Watson fumbled through her briefcase for copies of a methods class syllabus, a proposed clinical experience structure, and a list of student expectations, to give to the teachers. "Now," Dr. Watson began, "I know we may be pressed for time so I made copies of everything in the event we don't have time to go over everything." When Dr. Watson looked up, however, she could see the reluctance on the faces of all of the teachers. Backtracking quickly, Dr. Watson started again, expressing that she sensed some hesitancy on the part of the teachers and she really wanted to begin by establishing open communication. "Before we go on with all this paperwork," Dr. Watson said, "why don't we talk a bit about what you want to get out of working with me, and then I can explain a bit about where I am coming from with regard to preparing our undergraduates."

In response, one teacher stated that the physical education faculty were very concerned because they had learned that some Johnson Middle School teachers were being paid for mentoring clinical experience students and they were not. In addition, she asked "Since all teachers get paid to mentor student teachers, why should we, the physical education faculty, use our placements to mentor clinical experience students?"

Dr. Watson was at a loss for an answer to such a to-the-point question. It was clear to her that the physical education teachers at Johnson Middle School felt that they were not being treated fairly and believed they may be taken advantage of with this latest attempt at a working arrangement with the university. Dr. Watson quickly agreed that she would look into the matter and would attempt to work out an amenable compensation arrangement in the context of the requested clinical experiences. She then went on to briefly describe why she thought these pre–student teaching practical experiences to be so important. The teachers explained that it would have to be a departmental decision as to whether or not to take on clinical experience students and that a meeting with the entire physical education faculty would be necessary. Dr. Watson thanked everyone for their time, left her materials for the teachers to look over, and scheduled a meeting with the Johnson Middle School teachers for the following week.

Upon returning to her office, Dr. Watson telephoned the Associate Dean of the College of Education and informed her of the remuneration dilemma she had encountered at Johnson Middle School. The Associate Dean was not surprised. She explained that she was aware of this problem but at this point was not considering monetary exchange in the budget for the clinical experiences that had been mandated by the university advisory board. Dr. Watson knew that by next week she would have no clear answers to these difficult questions, but she remained committed to forging ahead.

The morning of the next teacher meeting, Dr. Watson arrived at Johnson Middle School well before the time of the meeting and found the same teacher waiting to greet her at the front door. They exchanged pleasantries and proceeded to one of the regular classrooms for the teacher meeting. Once there, Sally Smithers, the department head, explained that most of the teachers should be coming but would probably be a bit late. Dr. Watson used the opportunity to explain that she was working on a solution to the remuneration problem, but that as of today, she had no answers. She apologized sincerely, and told them that she promised answers to their questions soon. The teachers nodded, but Dr. Watson could tell they remained reluctant. Once most of the teachers had trickled in and taken a seat, Sally Smithers introduced everyone to Dr. Watson and explained the purpose of their meeting.

Dr. Watson thanked Sally Smithers, stood, and began distributing copies of papers that outlined how she foresaw the implementation and structure of a clinical experience tied to the university instructional methods class. She explained each handout and carefully explained how clinical experience students would be held accountable and evaluated. In addition, she explained that a university supervisor would be present during clinical experience once per week. Dr. Watson knew that she had raised an important issue when the teachers began to nod in approval. Dr. Watson continued to detail the student expectations materials in more detail, including how clinical experience students should dress, the schedule and time commitments involved, and related grade exchanges. She went on to explain her commitment to placing each student personally so as to be sure the schedules would match. Dr. Watson also emphasized the cooperative nature of the clinical experience evaluation and feedback and how important it was to facilitate community discussion among university supervisor, practicing teacher, and the preservice teacher to come to a shared sense of understanding regarding effective teaching practice. This type of information seemed to hit a positive chord with the teachers for, at the end of Dr. Watson's presentation, the teachers seemed less reluctant in posture and agreed to try such an experience for a semester to see how it might work out.

Dr. Watson left the meeting feeling relieved that she had succeeded in making an initial agreement with the teachers. She remained uncertain, however, as to how to overcome the remuneration challenge, which she could tell was pressing on the teachers' minds. Clearly, she would have to come to some sort of solution regarding how to compensate the teachers for their efforts.

The following week, Dr. Watson attended another university advisory board meeting where to her surprise the Associate Dean proposed that public school teachers involved in clinical experiences receive remuneration for clinical experience students. After much deliberation, the board elected to give each mentor teacher a stipend for each clinical experience student. Elated, Dr. Watson drove to Johnson Middle School to share the news with Sally Smithers. Dr. Watson could tell the news of the stipend made Sally Smithers more comfortable with her. With the clinical experience students scheduled to begin next week, Dr. Watson left her meeting with Sally Smithers knowing that if she was to make her initial partnership effort an ongoing success, and was to gain the professional trust of these teachers in the process, she would have to make every effort to implement the clinical experiences as she had stipulated in their first meeting together.

Ms. Sally Smithers

Sally Smithers moved to the community after teaching physical education for seven years in another rural community. Hired at Johnson Middle School, she was excited about the professional opportunities that might exist in a university town. She was also enthusiastic about the possibility of interacting on a regular basis with the faculty and students in the university physical education teacher education (PETE) program. She thought to herself that she was finally in a professional situation where she could look forward to the ongoing appreciation of committed public school educators. Operating on the assumption that university personnel would recognize and value effective public school teaching and a desire to work with the university programs, she was eager to roll up her sleeves and dig in to her new position at Johnson Middle School.

Ms. Smithers' first interaction with the university was a letter from Dr. Mann, the PETE program director at the university. The letter essentially inquired whether she would be interested in "mentoring" a university clinical experience student. The letter was unclear as to the responsibilities involved and did not specify any expectations on the part of the public school teacher or on the part of the university clinical experience student. Puzzled, Ms. Smithers asked one of her physical education colleagues, Mrs. Snow, what "mentoring" a university student would entail, assuming that Mrs. Snow had worked with Dr. Mann's students in the past. Mrs. Snow informed her that mentoring entailed the university student coming in and helping with one of her classes for ten hours over the course of a semester. Feeling a bit apprehensive, Ms. Smithers sent the request letter back agreeing to get involved in the clinical experience.

Putting her correspondence with Dr. Mann out of her mind, Ms. Smithers quickly became entrenched in the time-consuming and challenging task of teaching her classes on a daily basis. She worked hard to structure student experiences according to the principles she held important and to continually create and recreate lessons designed to excite students about physical education and related fitness and fair-play issues. As the semester wore on, Ms. Smithers was often overwhelmed by the many challenges of teaching and directing a quality physical education program. Trying to reach out to students to raise their self-esteem, advise students on a range of school and life issues, take a school and community leadership role in causes such as drug and disease prevention, work with the families of students at risk, and keep up with her physical education program responsibilities was quite a juggling act.

One morning, after attempting to solve some student challenges, a complete stranger showed up in one of her physical education classes. After Ms. Smithers got her students engaged in the lesson, she asked the woman how she could help. The woman told her that her name was Elaine, and that she was her clinical experience student from the university. Elaine asked Ms. Smithers when she could get a moment of her time to discuss her expectations. Elaine wanted to know what class period she would be visiting and how "it" would fit into her busy schedule. She wanted to know what activities and sports would be covered and gave the impression that she wanted Ms. Smithers to plan her experience right then and there. She additionally explained to Ms. Smithers that she was not familiar or comfortable with some sport activities and may not be able to help out with some things. Annoyed and somewhat shocked at this student's attitude, Ms. Smithers asked Elaine to meet with her during her prep hour so that she could focus solely on the needs of Elaine. Elaine explained that she was unable to meet during Ms. Smithers' prep hour. Ms. Smithers suggested before or after school times, but Elaine explained that those times were unacceptable as well. As an after school time could not be met, Ms. Smithers suggested that Elaine return to the university to figure out how to make some sort of schedule change to accommodate her clinical experience. When Elaine left, Sally began fuming to herself about the audacity of the university to simply dump a clearly unprepared and uncommitted student on a teacher without any warning.

After her encounter with Elaine, Ms. Smithers felt disappointed and frustrated with Dr. Mann's approach to working with public school teachers. She could not get past what she felt to be grave insensitivity on the part of the university program to give no previous warning and no structure or direction to what she felt to be an important educational experience in an undergraduate teacher education program. She wondered if this was how programs typically operate at the university, and if so, wondered whether to take part in this program.

A few days later, she received a phone call from Elaine. Elaine asked if it would be possible to meet her that day after school. Ms. Smithers had a committee meeting, but was willing to put off the meeting in order to make time for Elaine. At the meeting, Elaine produced a list of things she needed to accomplish during what would be a ten-hour clinical experience. The list included a host of items in very disjointed order, such as observe teaching; learn all students' names; plan and demonstrate a warm-up activity to students; teach a small group of students a particular skill; set up equipment; write a lesson plan and teach the entire class a skill; record test scores; contact a parent; correct papers; discuss questions with the class; and record grades. Ms. Smithers thought to herself that at least some information was coming from the university, but in the context of a ten-hour commitment the list of items to accomplish was ludicrous.

Ms. Smithers never directly received any assessment instructions from Dr. Mann, but was informed by Elaine that she needed to sign off on each item on the clinical experience list as it was accomplished. As the clinical experience progressed, the time constraint and lack of direction on the part of the university began to pressure both Elaine and Ms. Smithers. Ms. Smithers felt like she could not in good conscience sign off on many of the experiences contained on the clinical task list, but was unsure just how to navigate this challenge. Ms. Smithers also surmised that it would be difficult for Elaine to feel successful or that Elaine's experiences under her tutelage were perceived to be of value.

Ms. Smithers had progressed through the year with other clinical experience students and felt the same frustrations as she did with Elaine. While she was hoping for better communication with Dr. Mann, she wasn't quite sure just how to approach him and when she did, didn't feel that she was received very well. The following year there was a change at the university. Dr. Mann moved on to another position and another faculty member, Dr. Watson, replaced him. Shortly thereafter, Ms. Smithers received an introductory letter from Dr. Watson and reluctantly, she responded. Before long, Ms. Smithers received a telephone call from Dr. Watson. "It's only been a couple days since my response," Sally said to herself, encouraged by the prompt nature of this new faculty member. Their initial conversation ended by agreeing to meet together along with the rest of the physical education faculty at Johnson Middle School to discuss the clinical experience activities. Though hesitant based on her previous experiences with Dr. Mann, Ms. Smithers ended her day with optimism over the potential of working with the kind of university program she initially envisioned.

At the meeting Dr. Watson explained her program. She had made copies of a handout, which outlined her expectations and how she planned to implement the clinical experience. She carefully explained all aspects of the clinical experience. There was clear organization and structure and she addressed all problems Ms. Smithers was frustrated with the year before. When the meeting had ended all the teachers expressed to Ms. Smithers how much they appreciated Dr. Watson taking the time to explain her clinical experience to them personally. Ms. Smithers felt that this had made them all feel as though they were an important and equally contributing component of Dr. Watson's teacher education program.

Prior to this meeting, and on behalf of the rest of the physical education faculty, another teacher (Mrs. Snow) asked Dr. Watson why the teachers should accept clinical experience students without remuneration only to spend countless hours with them and then have them go to a different school to student teach under other teachers, who would be compensated accordingly. Additionally, Mrs. Snow had informed Dr. Watson that there were teachers in the English Department at Johnson Middle School who received remuneration for mentoring clinical experience students. Again at this meeting, Dr. Watson reassured both Mrs. Snow and Ms. Smithers that she would find answers to this question. "It seems to me that the university should ensure that the structure and compensation for clinical experiences should be the same across all departments," Dr. Watson said as she promised again to find answers. In any case, it appeared that Dr. Watson was hoping for a long-term commitment from the Johnson Middle School teachers to agree to work together over the clinical experience.

Ms. Smithers and the other teachers left their meeting with Dr. Watson with a reserved but altogether different impression than they had prior to the start of the meeting. Though Ms. Smithers was not convinced that Dr. Watson would actually follow through on the remuneration concern, she was now hopeful regarding the improved nature of the clinical experience activities and recognized potential for a more effective experience for the undergraduate students who would participate.

About a week later, Ms. Smithers was surprised by an unexpected visit from Dr. Watson at the school. With great enthusiasm, Dr. Watson explained that she had spoken with the Dean of the College, and the advisory board had approved a nominal teacher payment for clinical experience participation. Though clearly a token payment, Ms. Smithers thought to herself that perhaps this faculty member was actually going to follow through with the kinds of things she spoke of as important.

When the first of the clinical experience students came out to meet with Ms. Smithers, she was impressed that they arrived according to the schedule that Dr. Watson had prepared and sent out earlier, and that they were dressed appropriately. Ms. Smithers thought to herself that Dr. Watson must have talked to these students in detail and must really be following through with her initial plans. Each student clarified when they would be coming out for their next visit, just what their responsibilities would be when they arrived, and asked relevant questions in preparation for that next visit. Ms. Smithers left her initial meeting with these undergraduates feeling refreshed and hopeful that the types of activities and involvement she sought with a university teacher education program may actually come about.

As time went on, the clinical experience students continued to meet their assigned tasks as Ms. Smithers expected. Over time, Sally became comfortable that she and her clinical experience students would be able to meet all of the expectations set up by Dr. Watson. She was also appreciative of Dr. Watson's consistent presence at the school to reinforce expectations and to encourage a continued relationship with all of the other physical education teachers.

Throughout this clinical experience, Sally contemplated the new clinical experience program set up by Dr. Watson. She felt the important organizational changes she had made and the interpersonal touch that Dr. Watson gave to the program made it more effective. "Perhaps there is hope for a long-term relationship with Dr. Watson and her university program," she thought.

Questions

Preparing for Learning & Teaching

1. In your opinion, are school/university partnerships essential to effective teacher education programs? Why or why not?

2. Briefly describe the characters in this case and what they bring to the professional partnership.

3. What motivations did each participant have to establish a professional partnership?

4. What factors served as potential roadblocks in the development of this school/university professional partnership?

5. How were these roadblocks overcome?

6. This case is presented from two perspectives: that of a university professsor and that of members of a middle school physical education department. The university students participating in the clinical experience are also impacted by the scenario presented in this case. Role play this case from the perspective of the student Elaine and from the perspective of a student who will enter the clinical experience program after Dr. Watson assumes its management.

7. What elements are essential to the development and maintenance of any school/university professional relationship?

8. Distinguish the differences between the terms *cooperation, collegiality,* and *collaboration.* Discuss these terms and how they relate to schools and universities working with one another in teacher education.

9. In addition to a focus on undergraduate teacher education, what other types of school/university activities may result from such partnerships?

10. How may the additional activities you have listed in question 9 help facilitate the effectiveness of an undergraduate teacher education program?

ESL

Gayle E. Hutchinson

Claudia McKnight

Case 9

There is something marvelous about that first-day-of-school adrenaline rush. Rita was totally pumped as she drove to Crandall Elementary School. She had packed her car the night before with cones, poly spots, and hula hoops. Sleep? You must be kidding. She spent the night reviewing the lessons she had planned for today a thousand times. With the children in grades K–2, she will spend time on space awareness and selected locomotor skills like walking, running, sliding, hopping, and jumping. For children in grades 3–6, she will review general space and self-space quickly, while practicing locomotor skills. In all classes she will use the activities to practice student listening to start/stop signals and teacher directions.

As Rita was driving, she found herself reflecting on the extraordinary past month. She had shouted, "Yes!" when she thought about her selection as the first elementary physical education specialist in the Santiago School District. Four weeks of nonstop planning followed, meeting the school staff, plus ordering and gathering equipment. Rita's teaching schedule was divided between two schools; Monday and Wednesday at Crandall, Tuesday and Thursday at Mountain View. Fridays would be devoted to planning the next week's activities and organizing the lunchtime intramural sports program for grades 4–6, which she was to oversee at both campuses.

Rita was becoming discouraged. Children were chattering in at least three different languages and many of them were holding hands. Then, several unexpected things happened. First of all, they seemed to be having trouble "listening."

The superintendent picked the two most divergent schools in the district in which to initiate this physical education pilot program. Both schools were K–6 with approximately 600 students each; however, the demographics were opposite. Crandall Elementary students come from the most affluent neighborhood in town. The majority are white and their parents are very involved in their children's education. The Mountain View students are from the lower end of the economic spectrum. They are white, African-American, Asian-American, and Hispanic. Fifty percent are Limited English Proficient (LEP). If Rita's program works with these two divergent student populations, the district will hire three more specialists in June to cover an additional six schools the following year.

Crandall School was only two years old. The buildings were laid out in a pleasing mosaic. All the playground equipment was state-of-the-art. A beautifully maintained field space ran the length of the school. On the sides were hardtop areas the students used during recess and special activities. Rita even had access to the school cafeteria during inclement weather. Crandall had its equipment neatly stored in an equipment closet. Additionally, a new city park was adjacent to Crandall with a softball diamond, sand volleyball courts, and soccer fields.

Mountain View School, by contrast, was built in the early 1950s. As the area evolved from farmland into a hodgepodge of homes and apartments, more buildings were added. There were 12 permanent portable classrooms, which added to the jumble of buildings. The campus grounds were in a state of decline. There were cracks in the asphalt playing areas, and the field was full of ruts and bald spots. Rita was told the cafeteria was off limits during inclement weather because it was used to house spelling, reading, and math groups all morning and afternoon. The principal informed her that there was no space for her to store equipment. Even with these conditions, Rita was optimistic about creating a beneficial physical education program for her Mountain View students.

Rita pulled into the parking lot at Crandall School. Unloading her equipment into her collapsible cart, she was aware of the noises from the playground as the arriving students greeted each other and joined games. A voice behind her inquired, "Do you need some help?"

Turning around, Rita found three girls scanning all the equipment. "Yes, I do," she answered. In one trip they got it all stacked in the equipment closet. After the last bag was loaded in, Rita introduced herself to her helpers.

"I'm Ms. Thomas, your physical education teacher."

"I'm Cindy, and these are my best friends, Sarah and Autumn. We are in Ms. Bank's sixth-grade class."

"We are all in gymnastics together," added Sarah.

"Do we get P. E. today?" inquired Autumn.

"Yes, you do. Today I am going to do something with every class."

"Cool! We'll see you later," said Autumn.

With that, the girls went down the hall, greeting everyone they saw with shrieks of glee, as if they had been apart for years rather than one summer. What a wonderful way to start my first day, Rita smiled to herself.

Rita took the bag with the primary equipment and went to the first-grade playground. The teachers had all received their schedules a week ago when she had met with them at their staff meeting. Just as she finished setting up, along came 30 first graders, moving as only first graders can, like one giant amoebae. The next two hours were a blur, but she felt energized after working with four classes. Rita finally understood what had often been stressed in her methods classes; there are some things that one can only learn by doing, such as how difficult it is to get kindergarten children to actually follow two directions given at the same time. All things considered, she was pleased and excited. Her enthusiasm carried through the next two hours. All the students and teachers had been responsive. Every teacher helped out and followed Rita's directions.

The afternoon presented a new set of challenges. A sixth-grade class was the first class to arrive on the hardtop area. Thirty-four students walked behind a confident woman whom Rita recognized from the teachers' lounge. As she watched the youngsters approach, Rita was struck with how much taller and older they appeared than their primary counterparts. Once on the hardtop, the teacher gave a loud, short command, "Line up!" The students immediately formed six straight lines ranging from 4 to 6 students in each line, and sat down.

The teacher then turned to Rita, smiled, and said kindly, "Good luck. I'll be back in 40 minutes. If you have any problems, send them to me. I'll be in my classroom working."

Before Rita could thank her, the teacher had turned on her heels and walked quickly from the area. Rita watched for a moment, then turned to greet her new sea of faces, confident that she would be successful. As she began the lesson someone asked, "Why can't we just play football?" Rita ignored the remark and continued with her explanation of the lesson.

"This is dumb," came from the back of the group.

Rita had been forewarned about this age group by her last master teacher. "When complaining begins, ignore it and get them into your planned activity quickly." She momentarily lost her confidence, but kept enough presence of mind to move forward with her lesson. The complaining ended. It was very interesting to note that the least responsive class seemed to reflect their teacher's attitude. Physical Education wasn't important enough to stick around for and observe.

As Rita was loading the equipment back into her car, she realized she was exhausted. All that nervous energy she began the day with was spent. That evening she replayed the ups and downs of the day and decided the ups won. She went to bed too exhausted to be nervous about tomorrow, her first day at Mountain View School.

"Since this is Tuesday, this must be Mountain View School," Rita smiled to herself as she began unpacking her car. She was struck by the sound of the cars going past. What was wrong? There were no children's voices drifting from the playground. Then she remembered the children were not allowed on the playground before school; they either went to the cafeteria for breakfast or to the library to do homework. At 7:55 she heard a bell, and kids streamed out of the cafeteria and library, going straight to their classrooms.

Right on schedule, along came her first group of 32 first graders. She was struck by the sea of brown, black, yellow, and white faces that greeted her. Children were chattering in at least three different languages and many of them were holding hands. Then, several unexpected things happened. First of all, they seemed to be having trouble "listening." Her space activities were a failure, as many of the students would not let go of their friends' hands. Rita's start/stop signals were confusing to the children, and her directions were met with perplexed or blank looks. With the classroom teacher's help, she got through a third of her lesson. The same scenario was repeated with all her primary classes. By the end of the morning, Rita was becoming discouraged.

During lunch, Rita pondered the differences between the students' responses yesterday and today. She had set up all of her classes to begin with activities that would emphasize listening skills, identify self-space, and practice respectful, safe movement in general space. Although she had some problems in the morning, this approach really worked well yesterday. She believed, as she was taught in many teacher prep courses, that before her students could maximize opportunities for learning, she would have to create a safe learning environment. Establishing a safe and comfortable class for learning meant that students would listen when the teacher and others spoke. It meant that students would demonstrate self-control when moving in general and self-space. It meant that students would actively engage in all learning activities, treat equipment with respect, and be respectful and tolerant toward one another. She reflected on how to get all the kids to understand.

Rita's first group of fifth graders in the afternoon arrived ready to go. The teacher told her that the students were really excited. As Rita was explaining her expectations to the class, a boy in the back raised his hand. Before Rita could call on him he shouted, "When are we going to play a game?" When Rita explained that they would not play a game but engage in fun activities, someone else shouted, "That's not what we do in P. E. We usually play a game. It's fun." Hit with fear that she was losing another fifth-grade class, Rita scrambled to maintain their attention. Quickly she identified the boundaries that marked the large rectangular area where they would be working. Next, she briefly described the concept of self-space. As students explored their own self-space, Rita was struck again by the diversity of the class. Of the 30 students, 8 were Hmong, 6 Hispanic, 3 African-American, and the remaining 13 were Caucasian. She noticed that the Hmong students kept to themselves and spoke in their native language. The Hispanic children did the same.

Working in their own self-space involved all students. Rita noticed that she had to continually change the challenge in order to maintain student interest in the activity. When she called their attention to move on to activities in general space, the same boy in the back again asked, "When are we going to play a game?" Rita replied that we would not be playing a game, and heard someone quietly comment, "This is stupid." Rita chose to ignore that comment and continued with the lesson.

Rita explained that she would like to see students moving through general space using different locomotor skills. When she said, "Go," she noticed that many students were standing around. She stopped the class and explained it again, but the response was the same; many simply stood around and watched their classmates. Some students seemed to mimic other children's movements. Then it dawned on Rita that the students standing around were mainly Hmong and Hispanic. The classroom teacher arrived to take her students back to the classroom.

Rita was happy to have the class end. She was relieved that due to an assembly, this was the only class she had this afternoon. She now had a chance to reflect on what happened during the day. It seemed that the students with LEP in her classes did not understand her verbal directions.

As she was making notes on her first two days, Rita recalled the negative comments made by some of the boys at each school. She had to remind herself that out of the hundreds of children she had worked with, two or three complaints were not bad. Rita was more concerned with reaching the students with LEP. Some strategies came to mind and she decided to try them on Thursday.

Wednesday passed with no complaints. The Crandall kids knew the signals and were "in the routine." Rita had encouraged the students to ask questions, and they did. She thoroughly enjoyed her day.

On Thursday, she found herself repeatedly comparing her Mountain View students to her Crandall students, especially after she had "lost" the Mountain View kids while explaining a task. She tried speaking slower and louder but the students with LEP looked at each other, fidgeted, and often carried on quiet side conversations in Hmong or Spanish. Very few children, English speakers included, asked any questions. More often than not, when the children were released to do each task, part of the group had to be called back for corrections. When she tried to speak with the Hispanic or Hmong students, they would look down or away but never into her eyes. Rita felt they were avoiding her or not paying attention to what she was saying.

After school, Rita sought out the classroom teacher of the last group she had. "Mrs. Gonzales, may I ask you a question about some of the kids in your class?"

"They were not rude, were they?" Mrs. Gonzales responded.

"Well, I am not really sure. This is my first experience teaching children who are Hmong and Hispanic. When I asked them to look at me while I was speaking to them no one would. Since they all behaved the same way I assumed it was something cultural."

"You are very perceptive. It would be a sign of disrespect for any of those students to look you in the eye. The recent immigrants honor their cultural dictates regarding authority. Teachers are held in high esteem in both cultures. Be assured they are listening to you." Rita thanked Mrs. Gonzales and left feeling relieved.

Rita woke on Friday morning, exhausted from the week's activities but excited about beginning another phase of her program. Today would be the first day of the noon-time intramural program at both Crandall and Mountain View. Rita believed that if she started this activity program she would ensure that most students in grades 4–6 would be more active during the school week.

When Rita took the job she told the superintendent about her intramural plan. The superintendent thought it was a great idea and budgeted a small sum of money to pay for two college student interns to work five hours a week directly supervising the program at each school. Rita recruited two physical education majors in the last year of their program at the local state college. She met with Julio and Sandra several times to plan the noon-time intramural program. Together, the threesome determined how students would sign up for intramural; how they would create heterogeneous teams based on skill and gender; and how they would set up game-play with an emphasis on cooperation and fair play and less emphasis on winning and losing. Rita felt that they had created an "awesome" plan. They would implement this plan today. Flag football was the selected noon-time activity.

Rita worked at home from 8:00 A.M. to 9:30 A.M. planning her physical education classes for the following week. The minutes crawled by as Rita planned. She was too excited about the intramural program. At 10:00, she parked at Crandall where she was meeting Julio and Sandra. They were there before her, dressed in new sweat pants and warm-up jackets. She could tell by their smiles that they were excited too.

Entire classrooms signed up for intramural play. Each classroom had approximately 30 girls and boys who wanted to participate. Rita decided that a sports play intramural model would work well in this situation. Each class of 30 students was divided into five teams of six players each. Four teams from each class would engage in game play while the members of the fifth team served as officials and referees. Rita felt that teaching students how to officiate game play would help students take responsibility for their behavior and also reinforce game rules. It would also help Julio and Sandra who had to supervise a number of games during the noon hour. As students became more proficient at playing fairly and officiating accurately, Rita envisioned intraclass play. In other words, small teams from one fourth-grade class would play against small teams from another fourth-grade class.

Together they reviewed the sign-up sheets and the teams that they had created. Not knowing the students very well, they were concerned with whether or not these teams would be equitable. Rita felt strongly that the intramural program should focus on maximum participation by all students. Dividing each classroom into small groups would ensure that each student would have opportunities to be actively engaged in game play. Rita would oversee the functioning of the intramural program. Julio and Sandra would implement the program at each school.

Rita and Julio had not anticipated the extent of the grumbling they heard from some of the Crandall School fourth-, fifth-, and sixth-grade boys when their teams were announced.

"Why can't we pick our own teams? I think the boys and girls should be on separate teams like we are in the recreational leagues."

"Yeah, I'm with a bunch of losers."

"If you let us pick, we'll blow all the other teams away. Six of us are on real football teams, not this sissy flag stuff."

Rita answered each comment with, "This is just for fun." She helped Julio get everything started and then raced over to Mountain View School. As she drove, she wondered how Sandra was making out. Had she met with the same barrage of complaints?

At Mountain View the response was mixed. The majority of the students were okay with their teams. In a few cases there were comments about one team being the weakest or strongest in a class, but no complaints about mixing the genders.

Rita, Julio, and Sandra were discouraged by the students' performances at both schools. Overwhelmed with how to make the noon-time program a positive experience for the fourth to sixth graders, Rita, Julio, and Sandra took a collective deep breath and returned to the drawing board. They decided to reflect first on what happened individually at each school, then review commonalties among the two schools. They began with Crandall.

First, it was evident that the boys and girls at this predominately white school were used to doing things separately. This was difficult for Rita to understand since they were coed in most things at school. Then it dawned on her. Every Wednesday evening she played soccer in the town recreation league. On her way to the playing field, Rita always passed youth leagues playing or practicing. The soccer and softball leagues were separated by gender. Rita also realized that the football league was only for the boys. The girls participate as cheerleaders during football season. Rita thoughtfully exclaimed, "No wonder boys and girls don't know how to play together. That's not the way they have been socialized when it comes to athletics."

The events at Mountain View were very different. The students were preoccupied with who would be on their team. They seemed to want the best athletes to play with them. Interestingly, it did not matter if the most skilled was a boy or a girl. What mattered was their perceived level of performance during game play. As Rita, Sandra, and Julio discussed this observation, no one knew why this occurred.

Then there was the separate issue of officiating. At Crandall, those who considered themselves "jocks" were whistle happy. Every possible penalty was called. When students grumbled, they were ejected from the game. The situation at Mountain View was not as vindictive as at Crandall; rather it was "organized confusion." Some violations were called inappropriately, although seldom objected to, depending on the level of English proficiency of the team officiating. Verbal charges of incompetence were hurled freely. Responses were often in raised voices in mixed English, Spanish, or Hmong. It was obvious to the adult supervisors that knowledge of the rules was lacking among the students at both sites.

Sandra and Julio seemed to grow more discouraged as they pondered the situation before them. Rita was pacing when suddenly "the light went on." She was beginning to realize the true complexity of the student body at each school. The students at Crandall were a homogeneous group in terms of ethnicity, language, and socioeconomic background.

However, they were diverse in terms of gender and level of motor skill. The students at Mountain View were a heterogeneous group. They represented different gender, culture, motor abilities, and languages. In fact, many students did not speak English and were not aware of the cultural nuances embedded in American sport and game play.

As Rita explained her thinking to the others, a plan formulated. First she would determine a cross-cultural sport with which most students and both genders were familiar.

"Soccer?" suggested Julio.

"Perfect," Sandra answered.

"I will work on striking and kicking with soccer and playground balls in my physical education classes. We will focus on kicking, dribbling, passing, dodging, and tackling," exclaimed Rita.

It was decided that they would modify the noon-time intramural games each week so that they focused on a specific skill and movement concept practiced during the school week. Rita would also continue helping students move comfortably through general and self-space. She also was determined to help students learn cooperative and respectful behaviors that would encourage them to play fairly.

Rita talked Julio and Sandra into volunteering more of their time in order to spend 30 minutes in each class each week discussing game rules and jargon specific to game play, as well as skills for officiating. All three believed that helping the students understand the rules and giving them practice in officiating skills would help them play more fairly and cooperatively on Fridays. When Rita explained her new plan to the building principals and classroom teachers, they heartily approved.

Rita now approached her job at each school with a clearer understanding of her pupils. At Crandall, her emphasis was on mixing the genders and improving each student's skill level. At Mountain View, she had to find an instructional approach that would clearly communicate to her LEP students what she was teaching. This challenge had never been presented in her teacher preparation courses. She was born, raised, and educated in a town that had a small minority population, but everyone spoke English at school. To gain the necessary mentoring, Rita contacted two primary teachers at Mountain View and arranged to visit their classrooms on Friday morning.

During the week, Rita took notes on what did and did not work. She noted that the students in the primary grades at Crandall were totally involved in all the skill theme and movement activities that she did. The older students did well on the skill theme and modified sport skill activities, but she knew it was going to take time to overcome the gender bias. However, she was able to identify the outspoken students and would focus on their behaviors.

Rita's first classroom observation took her into Mr. Murphy's class. Mr. Martin Murphy had been teaching for five years. He graduated from the same college as Rita. This was his first year at Mountain View School, and he exclaimed that he "loved it, particularly working with Limited English Proficient children." Rita noticed immediately the colorful classroom walls filled with the children's work—posters, pictures, and children's art. The ambiance was cheerful and inviting.

It was five minutes before class time and most of the second-grade children were already in their seats putting things away, reading, or visiting quietly. Martin greeted Rita with a captivating smile and asked her to sit in a chair next to Choua. She smiled at Choua and said, "Hello." She detected a faint smile, as Choua immediately lowered her eyes. Rita reached out to touch Choua on the head as a way to give a friendly greeting but stopped herself short. Last week in the teachers' lounge, she and Martin had engaged in a long conversation about cultural differences. She remembered Martin commenting on the Hmong culture. Touching children on the head was something that adults in America do to demonstrate friendliness, but in Hmong culture it was a serious reprimand to a child. Rita shuddered as she thought of the distress she could have caused Choua. Rita's reverie was interrupted by the sound of Martin's voice starting class.

Rita sat down to observe as Martin took an animated position in front of the class. She noticed there were 38 desks and 34 students present today. Martin had told her last week that of the 38 students in his class, 12 were Hmong, 15 were Hispanic, and 11 were Caucasian. One Hmong child was fluent in English, and the rest ran the gamut from non–English-speaking to limited English-speaking students. The same was true of the Hispanic students, and most were also limited in their understanding of English. Martin was able to understand and speak enough Spanish to be of some help to his Spanish-speaking students, but he knew no Hmong.

Science was the first lesson of the day. Martin had the children continue their work with the concept of classification. At the front of the room on a table was a large basket of fruit. Rita noticed a number of apples, oranges, pears, bananas, and peaches. Then, Martin held up three large cards. The first read "apple"; the second read "banana"; the third read "orange." Martin asked for volunteers to hold each card. Several hands went up immediately. "The first card reads 'apple.' Class, what does it say?" To Rita's surprise, the class together said, "Apple." "The first card, which reads 'apple,' shall go to Juanita. Juanita, what does the card read?" Juanita replied with a giant smile, "Apple." Martin exclaimed, "Very good, Juanita! Class?" Again, in unison the class said, "Apple." Martin continued to place the cards with eager students. Each time he repeated this dialogue with the class. It sounded very much like a rehearsed script with the tempo of a chant.

As Rita looked around the room, she was amazed at the concentration on each child's face. Even Choua was leaning forward in her chair and calling out the words loudly. Once the cards were placed with students, Martin went to the giant fruit basket. He pointed at it much like a talk-show host displays consumer products and said, "This is a fruit basket. Class, what is this?"

"A fruit basket!" was the enthusiastic response.

"Everyone, what is kept in the fruit basket?" challenged Martin with a smile. "Fruit!" came a tickled response from 34 students, who giggled at the question.

Rita observed Martin as he asked these questions and encouraged a unified response. It was obvious that he was monitoring each and every student's involvement and ability to make the appropriate reply. When it appeared that a student was unsure or did not understand, Martin asked the class to say it again, or several more times. If a student remained lost or confused after several group responses, Martin moved his way over to that student and helped him or her say it correctly. Rita was impressed with how he used visual aids, simple vocabulary, and group responses.

The second class she entered was Mrs. Anderson's first grade. She had 32 students, 16 of which were Limited English Proficient. She was presenting a science lesson. All of the students were gathered on the carpet in front of a magnetic chalkboard. She had a picture of a daisy growing in a flower pot. First, Mrs. Anderson said the name of each part and then had the class repeat it after her. Then she asked the students specific questions about each part while she pointed to them. "What does the pot do? That's right, it holds dirt. Now class, what does the pot do?"

"It holds dirt," came a chorus of voices.

Next Mrs. Anderson took cutouts of each section and called on a student to come up and put the flower pot up on the magnetic board, then the flower stem, then the flower. Then she took from behind her desk a real daisy growing in a flower pot. It was greeted with "Aah"s. She had a tray ready for each table with an empty flower pot, some potting soil, and a small daisy. She showed the class how to plant, step-by-step. They all did it together, first the teacher, then the students.

Rita was fascinated. She checked her notes; visual aides, choral responses, tactile involvement. All the students were engaged throughout the entire lesson. She briefly discussed the lesson with Mrs. Anderson, who commented wisely, "The bottom line, Rita, is to have a definite focus and keep it simple when first introducing a concept. I have also found that the choral response gives me immediate feedback on whether the children are understanding the content, and it prevents kids from 'tuning out.' These strategies work across all grade levels when you are teaching students with LEP."

It became evident to her that each child should have an opportunity to see, hear, touch, and speak the words in order to learn words, skills, or concepts. Instantly, Rita began transferring these instructional strategies to her physical education curricula.

After a week of observations, talking with classroom teachers who worked closely with LEP children, and replanning her lessons for students at Mountain View, Rita experienced a sense of relief and gratitude. Her content would remain the same. She would still teach and have students practice skill themes and movement concepts in K–6, with upper grade levels beginning to combine skills and engage in modified sport games and activities. However, she would alter her instructional strategies to include a lot of visuals, choral responses, reciprocal teaching, and tactile experiences. She would work to keep her demonstrations simple and consistent. Once again, Rita felt more confident in her ability to meet the needs of students with LEP.

Name   Date

Preparing for Learning & Teaching

1. Identify the critical issue in this case.

2. Rita decided that she "had to find an instructional approach that would clearly communicate to her students with LEP what she was teaching." How did Rita learn more about teaching LEP students? How can you learn more about teaching students with LEP?

3. What instructional strategies did Martin Murphy and Mrs. Anderson use with their students with LEP?

4. What are some of the specific elements that contribute to Limited English Proficiency?

5. What was the primary focus of the physical education program at Crandall and Mountain View Elementary Schools?

6. Review the demographics and facilities at both Crandall and Mountain View. How can two schools in the same town have such divergent demographics and facilities?

7. Why did Rita, Julio, and Sandra decide not to offer flag football as a noon-time activity?

8. What were the primary purposes of the noon-time intramural program?

9. How would you design and implement a noon-time intramural program to maximize student involvement and cooperation?

10. What other related topics and questions are raised by this case?

11. Discuss strategies for dealing with these issues.

Marginalization of P.E.

Sandra A. Stroot

Christine Bell

Carol Jones

Case 10

"Do you need any help, Ms. Alexander?" Krystee exclaimed as she scampered up from Latchkey. "Oh, are we going to use those streamers in our class today?" She was wide-eyed, with a toothless grin spreading from ear to ear as she took the streamers to help.

"Yes, your class will be using them today in your pathway lesson," answered Ms. Alexander. It was before 8:00 A.M. on Monday, and Ellen was amazed, as always, how active elementary children could be. This seemed to be especially true of the children in the Latchkey program, who sometimes arrived as early as 7:00 A.M.! "How wonderful to always be so excited," she thought, as she smiled at Krystee.

When Ellen arrived at Lakeside Elementary, there were only a few cars in the parking lot. Even though she did not have to be there until 8:50, she had many things to do to prepare for her classes. Ellen was excited to start her movement unit with the primary students. She had made new music tapes over the weekend to make the unit more exciting for them. She had also wanted to tape shapes and pathways onto the floor to help students learn the different themes. As Ellen was placing the tape on the floor, students started to come in from the fifth-grade classes. They were getting everything ready to choose teams for their soccer unit tomorrow. Ellen gave them the names of her students, the rules for choosing teams, and told them

Ellen went into the gym to rewind her music tapes for her afternoon primary lessons. As she walked in, she saw Mr. Jackson, the custodian, putting the last of the chairs on the floor of the gym for the afternoon assembly. "Oh no," thought Ellen. "Now what!"

to think about what they were going to do in the morning, as there would not be time to figure it out tomorrow. She told them that if they had any questions, she would be at school all morning and they could stop in at recess or after school.

Ellen went back to taping the floor, and two students came back to ask her about the number of students on a team. Ellen explained again that the entire class would be included, and they would need to divide the number of class members by the number of teams to get the answer. The students left with a grin on their faces, and Ellen finished her taping. It was already 8:40, and Ellen still wanted to get the primary warm-up tape changed to focus more on the upper-body muscle groups. It would only take a minute. She had compiled it last week, but she just could not seem to get that free minute!

Ellen hurried to get the correct warm-up tape. From the equipment room, she began to roll out the cart with the attendance books and tape player on it. The posters of shapes and pathways were ready to put along the walls in the gym. Ellen had learned a long time ago not to leave anything hanging in the gym, because the "after-school crowd" of basketball players had a tendency to rip the paper or write obscenities all over the posters. Jim Adams, the second-grade teacher, came into the gym just as Ellen was reaching for the posters.

"Ellen, are you in here?"

"Yes, I'm back in the equipment room. I'm glad you came in. Can you reach this poster? It fell back behind the cones, and I'm just not tall enough to get it."

Laughing, Jim reached the poster, and handed it to Ellen. "I came in to tell you that we are going on a field trip today, and I wondered if my class could come in with Mrs. Massey's first-grade class an hour early. Then my students wouldn't miss their gym time."

"Oh Jim, I don't think that will work. I'll have over 50 students in the gym. There is no way I can begin to teach my objectives, and besides, that many students in the gym is just not safe. Can they come in at 1:30 tomorrow instead? I can switch my conference period. Next time, if you'll come to me first before you need to change the schedule, I promise I'll help work out a solution that will be good for both of us."

"O.K. Ellen. I'll just bring them in tomorrow then. Thanks for working with us, and I'll try to think ahead a little better next time," he replied with a grin.

"Oh, no," thought Ellen, as she glanced at the clock. Her first class would be here any minute! She was so busy this morning she hadn't even had a cup of coffee.

Her class came in just as she put the new warm-up tape in the tape player. The morning classes went well, and Ellen was pleased with the student responses to her new music tapes and marks on the floor. The floor tape, posters, and music helped the students understand the different movement themes. She was glad she put in the extra work to make her lessons run more smoothly.

After her morning classes, Ellen quickly rolled her equipment cart back into the locked equipment room before leaving the gym. Ellen felt lucky that her physical education classes didn't have to be held in the eating area, like some physical education teachers' classes. Ellen was assigned lunch room or recess duty almost every day of the week. She hurried to playground duty, and as usual, all went well. The new peer mediation program was working well, and student arguments and conflicts were decreasing. Mr. Agnew, the new principal, worked hard to support the peer mediation program. He had some good ideas and seemed to work well with the teachers in the school.

After her playground duty, Ellen went into the teachers' lounge to eat her lunch. Mr. Agnew came in and reminded everyone that there was a school meeting the next day after school and that he would like to have the teachers there to discuss some important business. Ellen remembered that she had to go to Jefferson Elementary School tomorrow but made a note to get back to Lakeside for the meeting.

Mr. Agnew sat down next to Ellen, and started talking about his golf game. They were joking about hitting the ball in the water, and some of the other teachers started teasing Mr. Agnew about having more of his golf balls in the water than on the green. A call over the intercom system interrupted, and Mr. Agnew had to return to his office.

Ellen finished her lunch and was on her way to the gym when Mr. Agnew stopped her in the hall. "Ellen, remember, I called an assembly for this afternoon for the drug awareness group to meet with the fourth- and fifth-grade students. We will have to use the gym at 2:00. You won't mind moving your classes outside, will you?"

Ellen replied, "I remember, Mr. Agnew. I saw it in the weekly bulletin. I will have my primary classes finished by 2:00 and will take the third graders outside to begin soccer. No problem."

Ellen went into the gym to rewind her music tapes for her afternoon primary lessons. As she walked in, she saw Mr. Jackson, the custodian, putting the last of the chairs on the floor of the gym for the afternoon assembly. "Oh no," thought Ellen. "Now what!"

"Mr. Jackson, I am supposed to use the gym until 2:00. I still have two primary classes before the assembly. Can we move the chairs to the sides of the gym? I will help you, and if we hurry, we can get them off in time for the first graders to begin."

"Sorry, Ms. Alexander. Mr. Agnew told me to set them up now. Maybe you should talk to him first."

Ellen hurried to Mr. Agnew's office, and luckily he was in. She said, "Mr. Agnew, did you forget that I still have two classes in the gym before the assembly?"

"No, Ellen, I just wanted to make sure we were prepared ahead of time for the drug awareness group, in case we have parent visitors who want to see the assembly. They'll need a place to sit, and it is a nice day, so I thought you could take the students outside."

Ellen was shocked that Mr. Agnew would make that assumption. She reminded him that she was teaching a movement lesson and needed space as well as music and taped patterns on the floor. "Can we use the library or one of the fourth- or fifth-grade classrooms for parents who arrive early?"

"No, Ellen. I want everything to be ready for the assembly and not have everyone rushing around at the last minute setting up chairs. I'm going to have to ask you to give up your gym this afternoon. I'm sorry."

Ellen went back to the gym feeling frustrated by Mr. Agnew's request that she give up the gym. "I bet he wouldn't ask another teacher to give up their classroom," she thought, angrily! "I guess we could do some of the cooperative activities I was planning for next month, but I wanted to have the students learn the movement themes first so we could use them in the cooperative activities." Ellen finished the classes that afternoon by taking the students outside to review playground games, and she left still feeling angry and frustrated.

Ellen arrived at 7:45 on Tuesday morning. She had a lot to do, so she hustled out to paint the field, only to find that the can of paint was clogged and would not spray. Ellen had to run back into the school to get another can. Deciding to test it in the trash can, she managed to spray herself with white paint. That was par for the course, since every warm-up suit she owns has spray paint on it somewhere. It took about 25 minutes to measure and line the field for soccer. Ellen gathered eight students to help carry the four goals out to the field. She could always count on students to help, especially if they received a treat in return. They finished setting up by 8:45, so Ellen stopped in at the teachers' lounge for a quick cup of coffee.

The lounge was full, and Ellen said her usual good mornings as she poured her cup of decaf. The 8:50 bell rang, signaling that students could enter the school and their classrooms. Ellen made her way to the gymnasium to meet her 24 captains—4 per class. The captains got to work quickly choosing their teams from the list of students Ellen had provided for them and then headed to class. Ellen quickly rolled out her cart with the tape deck, attendance book, and other items she needed for classes. She also hung up the rules poster.

At 9:10, her fourth-grade class arrived and began warm ups with a boundary line jog and a stretching routine at their home bases. Class finished at 10:00 and was followed by two other 50-minute classes. After the fifth graders left, Ellen was ready for her lunch break. She quickly put away the equipment and slid the goals into the equipment room. Then the stations for the afternoon's first and second classes were set up. This took about 10 minutes of her lunch time, leaving 20 minutes to quickly eat, use the restroom, and check the mailbox before she had playground duty. There was a message to call a parent—she would have to wait until after school to return the call. The students on the playground had been reasonably well behaved today—thank goodness.

Ellen's duty officially ended at 12:35; however, the next teacher did not come out until 12:40, weakly apologizing that she lost track of time. Ellen replied that she understood but hoped that the class she was to teach was also late as she ran in quickly. Upon entering the gym, she saw that her second-grade students had already begun their warm-up jog around the boundary lines and Mrs. Funter, the homeroom teacher, was waiting patiently for Ellen to arrive. Ellen apologized and explained that she could not leave the playground until the next duty teacher arrived and thanked the teacher for starting the warm-ups. Mrs. Funter replied that she just asked the students what they were supposed to do and they did it. Ellen was pleased that her students knew the routine!

Ellen's next class was a group of first graders. She lined the students up promptly at 2:25, so they would be ready for the classroom teacher—who was late. Ellen only had 15 minutes to make it to her next class at another elementary school. So while the students played "paper, scissors, rock," she quickly rolled out the cart and put the equipment by the equipment room door. As soon as the teacher picked up the class, Ellen zoomed into action. She put all of the equipment away, gathered her belongings, shut the door, turned out the lights, and locked the gym door. On her way out to the car, she noticed that the music teacher was also late. At least she would not be the only traveling teacher to be late today.

"Misery loves company," she laughed as she climbed into the car. On to Jefferson Elementary, about eight minutes away on a good day. Ellen rushed to get into the building quickly. "What will happen when it snows and the roads are bad?" she wondered.

The class was just coming down the hall, so she just beat them to the gym. Susie Anthony, the full-time physical education teacher at the building, was just dismissing her class and greeted Ellen with a smile. She was always pleasant and willing to help.

"A bit rushed today," Susie said.

"Of course. Isn't that normal for me?" Ellen replied with a grin. Ellen quickly got the tape player and attendance book out of the office drawer and placed it on the stage as her class entered the gym. She'd have to get out the equipment after attendance and as the students warmed up at their home bases. Ellen knew that she was taking a chance by running into the equipment room, but while the students finished stretches she would duck in quickly.

When the class ended at 3:30, Ellen had to rush to put all the equipment away and hop back into the car. She really had to try to beat the buses out of the parking lot to make the scheduling meeting back at her home school. As she pulled out of the lot, she breathed a sigh of relief—she made it!

Although it was a real effort to get back to school, Ellen thought it was important to attend all meetings. The school district had decided two years ago that they would go to site-based management, where decisions regarding scheduling, school budget, policy, and such were to be made by teachers and administrators at each school building rather than by the district administrators. Ellen wanted to participate in these decisions to make Lakeside School the best in the district. She worked hard to make sure the students received a good education, and she knew the other teachers in her school were highly committed as well. Ellen thought site-based management was a good idea and was looking forward to working with her colleagues and new school principal.

She arrived only a few minutes late to the meeting. The members of the scheduling committee represented each grade level as well as related arts and special education teachers. They had begun to discuss the problem of the addition of another first-grade class to the school. Because of the large class sizes, the school board had voted to add another first-grade teacher and divide the three existing classes into four. Ellen had entered in the middle of the discussion. She could not believe what she was hearing!

"We think that the new first-grade class will fit nicely into the time of your preparation period on Tuesdays, Ellen," the chairperson said.

Astonished, Ellen replied, "What do you mean the time of my preparation period? When am I supposed to have my planning time?"

"Well, we've looked over the related arts schedule and you have 15 minutes of free time in the morning before school and 15 minutes after school that you can use for your planning time," she answered without hesitation.

Frustrated, Ellen rebutted, "But all teachers have that time before and after school. It is general supervision time for all teachers!"

Annoyed, the chairperson snapped, "But they are classroom teachers, and they have to be in their rooms preparing for students."

Tears welled up in Ellen's eyes as she thought, "And what was I doing this morning?"

Name   Date

Preparing for Learning & Teaching

1. What is the critical issue in this case?

2. Make a list of the managerial tasks that Ellen had to complete before classes began on Monday, the first day. On Tuesday. Between classes and schools. After school. What does this list tell you about Ellen's schedule?

3. Can you identify some of the ways Ellen is working with the rest of the school staff to meet the overall school needs?

4. Do you think Ellen is a good teacher? Why or why not?

5. Can you identify any incidents in this case that lead you to think the students, staff, and administrator(s) at Ellen's school value physical education?

6. Can you identify any incidents in this case that lead you to think the students, staff, and administrator(s) at Ellen's school marginalize physical education?

7. Why was Ellen so upset at the end of the staff meeting? If you were in Ellen's situation, what would you do?

8. What are the related issues and questions raised by this case?

9. What strategies might you use to address these issues?

Coworker Conflict II

Peg Nugent

Nell Faucette

Helene Hughes

Case 11

S o, you're our new coach," roared Alex, a power-packed body builder who tested the limits of spandex with each step. "I wondered who Chris would pick as my new partner. You'd think a principal would consult with you first, huh?" Alex shrugged and laughed, "From the looks of you, you can't lift much. And you sure weren't a linebacker. But we'll get along just fine. I get along with everybody. Everyone loves this ol' coach."

Brett trembled as thoughts began to swirl. "Be quiet! Don't rock the boat on your first day. Remember, successful collaboration is critical!" Brett tensed as Alex, without taking a breath, continued. "I know you have ideas to share with me. I was full of myself, too, when I first started 15 years ago. Well, I'm looking forward to learning from you. Why, we'll be colearners together. A prize-winning team. That'll be us. And Chris, our principal, loves that 'learning community' thing, too."

Brett began to relax. Maybe the first impression was wrong. Perhaps the two physical educators could share ideas and help each other. Brett smiled, saying, "I can't wait to talk with you about the model I used during my internships. It's designed to help develop every child at appropriate psychomotor, cognitive, and affective levels. It's one of the models our district adopted a couple of years ago. You know, they want children to be more self-directed,

> "What makes you think you're so much more committed or giving than I am? I get the sense you don't approve of me or my program. In fact, I don't think you've considered a thing that I do worth squat. Tell me, Brett, what gives you that right?"

accept responsibility, express feelings and ideas, while improving the quality of their psychomotor skills, and this model really helps."

"Whoa, young 'un! I'm open, but I'll need some time to adjust to those ivory tower gems. In the meantime, we'd better get down to real life and get ready for tag relay or dodgeball before the kids begin to swarm. Do you have a preference, Coach?"

Brett reddened and wondered, "Are these feelings of frustration or disbelief?" The thoughts roared, "I'm not a coach. I'm a teacher—a physical educator like my great-grandmother and someone from every succeeding generation in my family. I don't want to be 'Coach' for Alex, the principal, or the students." Brett paused, thinking, "Maybe I should wait 'til lunch to bring this issue up. I don't want to start out on the wrong foot with Alex."

The first-year teacher hustled to the equipment room thinking, "Should I attempt to model modified dodgeball for Alex, which helps reduce danger and increase student activity levels, or should I just keep quiet and follow for today?" The words of the university program coordinator stung in memory: "If you cannot get along, you'll never make it. One of the primary attributes needed for success is the ability to work collegially with everyone at your school." Brett was beginning to feel queasy.

As Brett neared the field, the voices of students rang loudly.

"What are we going to play today, Coach?"

"Can we play kickball? I'm the captain! No, you can't be on my team."

"Only Dream Team players for me. C'mon Jeff and Jimmy. Hey, Danny, you too. Forget it, Carmen. You, too, Angel and Reggie!"

As the children jostled, Alex whispered conspiratorially to Brett, "Give them lots of choices. That's one of the best teaching strategies out there. Even the ivory tower folks agree. Teaches kids responsibility. So I let them choose teams every time. Bet you didn't think I understood some of these newfangled ideas, huh?"

For the second time in 20 minutes, Brett's stomach fluttered as the new teacher thought back to a practice learned so recently: "Giving students choices is valued because they can learn to feel greater ownership while developing an understanding of choice consequences." Brett hesitated, thinking, "I know that this is not what my university professors meant about varying levels of choice."

Brett surveyed the asphalt court. Boys were teamed against each other in roughhouse play. Girls were shoved to the perimeter where they were arguing about force because the dodgeball was too painful. Three students and an aide were sitting or lying in a circle on the court with no equipment or apparent purpose. Alex had explained earlier that this group had learning disabilities so there was no need to worry about them. Other students, from varying ethnic or racial groups, were playing on the field. However, they seemed to be constructing a more advanced game than dodgeball. Brett was impressed both with their skill levels and interesting rules.

"I told you to forget that fancy stuff, boys!" yelled Coach Alex. "I'm tired of your showing off and refusing to tow the line. You're in time-out for the rest of this class. Maybe next time, you'll make choices that let me know you're listening."

Diego, Rashad, and their friends sulked over to the yellow line. Along the way, they back-flipped, moon-walked, and karate-kicked at their anger, thinking, "No one wanted us in, so why can't we just play soccer with each other?"

Brett's mind began racing again: "I've seen more undesirable behaviors, teaching strategies, and program goals in 10 minutes than I saw during three internships. I've got to talk to someone. I bet the principal would know how to help."

Brett's thoughts were shattered by the sound of Alex's booming. "Hey, you look wiped out and it's your first day. That's the problem when there's no access to the rigors of football or weight lifting at those wimp schools. But don't worry. I'll get you into shape fast. Pretty soon, you'll have 'buns of steel' too." "I know," Alex continued. "Let's talk to the principal. Maybe I can find a third ticket to the Noles–Gators game. You'll be able to be hang around with a couple of real jocks, that way! That should inspire you to toughen up!"

Bile leapt to Brett's throat. The principal and Alex were friends, Alex being the provider of Seminole tickets for the pair. Walking toward Chris's office to inquire about tickets, they rounded the corner and met Chris who, with a big pat on Alex's back, said, "How lucky you are, Brett, to be working with a professional like Alex who has given so much to this school during the past 15 years!"

Brett's image of a heart-to-heart dialogue with the principal exploded and new thoughts began to emerge: "I'm in deep trouble. If I can't last a year, my future is zip. This is my first day, and I can hardly keep my breakfast down. What can I do to make it until May when transfers become possible?"

After a tough night with little sleep, Brett's thoughts were interrupted.

"Let's go honey, you're running late," said Morgan. In the predawn hours of Brett's second day, the young teacher sighed and said glumly, "I don't think I can make it today—maybe never. It's not what I expected."

Morgan shuddered, "Don't even think about it. You're going! You gave up almost everything to get here. You believe in yourself and children. You believe you can help them. You can't let an overbearing colleague destroy your dream."

"I know what you're trying to do and I appreciate it," responded Brett, "but it seems hopeless to me. My principal just 'rewarded' me with a new title, Program Coordinator. Now I'm responsible for all elements of the program, including unit and lesson plans, which Alex calls ticker tape."

Morgan responded quickly, "Do you think you could look more positively at this? Maybe your principal just believes in you like I do!"

"You don't understand, Morgan," said a crestfallen Brett. "This means I'm in charge of equipment inventory, and there are no locks on the storage rooms. Plus, I'll have to do all the administrative reports for the state, the district, and the school. Worse, they've named me Patrol Coordinator, which means another hour at Alachua each day. That means I'll have to give up my afternoon job as a volleyball coach." Brett continued, "But worst of all, I am in the position of having to choose between 'getting along'—which seems to matter enormously to everyone—and 'doing the right thing,' as I understand it from my training. I'm at a loss."

Brett's second-day greeting from Alex was as unnerving as the first. "You look a little green around the gills, buddy. Out partying last night? Got to give that up now that you're in the real world with real demands and professionals. Ah, c'mon. Chin up. Be a marine!" welcomed Alex as the new colleague entered.

Brett breathed deeply and asked, "Would you be willing to talk to me about my feelings today, Alex? I'm having a really hard time, and I don't know if I have chosen the right field." Alex locked on intently and thought, "I could chew this puppy up if I wanted to!" Instead, the coach responded quietly, "Go ahead kid, what's on your mind?"

"I don't know if I have been living in a world of 'gobbledegook,'" said Brett, "or if what I learned might be of help to students, but I would like to find out. I know you have had years of experience, which I respect, but I would like to try what I've learned, if that would not create problems for you."

Alex reeled, thinking, "This kid's not as big a wimp as I thought. What the heck! Every dog's gotta have its day." Alex then said, "I'll tell you what. Why don't you let me do my thing cause it's hard to teach an old coach new tricks. But you go ahead and try out what you've been taught. It may be too much for me to do, but if you can help children, I'll be your number one fan!"

Nine weeks later, Alex seemed enthusiastic about the beginning teacher's success with the students, saying, "Well, Brett, you've made it through August and September and you're doing just fine! You've got them standing at attention and marching to your drum. In fact, I see that your kids are more active than a wind chime in a hurricane. Maybe we could team our classes so I could learn some of your activities and teaching strategies. I know a lot about getting kids under control, but you seem to have a knack for getting them involved and excited. I'm impressed!"

Brett mused, "Maybe I could help Alex learn to use this model along with some of the practices designed to increase student activity time. If we could share goals and program vision, we may be able to turn things around here. On the other hand, 60 to 70 students during each class with a colleague who knows little about what I'm trying to do. Wow, that could be deadly."

Alex interrupted Brett's thoughts, "I know. You be in the lead. I'll watch you like a hawk so I can learn. You can plan the lessons and units, so they'll progress well." Alex went on, "My kids sure can't keep their eyes off those juggling scarves you're using now. If my kids could join in, then I'll work all the controls to prevent bad behaviors from cropping up. What do you say? That way we'll be team teaching."

Brett knew that team teaching could be a win or lose proposition. It could be fun and stimulating to have a partner to work with during planning phases, or planning could become a nightmare with two different opinions being expressed about everything from curricular objectives and program goals to content and class management strategies. That could mean ongoing conflict. Then again, Brett remembered, "Alex detests lesson planning and jokes about it as 'infant activity' instead of 'instant activity,' so conflict might not be such a problem in that respect."

Brett also knew that sharing equipment could become an issue though; currently, the new teacher only got leftovers anyway. Brett imagined how it might be working with a teammate who also wanted to create an exemplary partnership and program for their elementary school. Brett would give it a go.

Brett gave his class instructions to pick a partner with whom they hadn't worked before. "Today, you and your partner will explore communication as a theme. You're going to give specific feedback to your partners about how they are performing the skill to help them improve."

Having completed instant activity designed for fitness, warm-up, and movement onto the court, the second graders were sitting in a circle at full attention. They knew that demonstrations would be next and they were ready. After all, the camera was rolling and they might be featured the next day on the school's morning TV program. Most of the kids felt it was an honor to be featured as an outstanding student during their principal's daily television welcome.

The students' visions of grandeur were shattered as Alex swooped down on them, shouting, "Heads up. Eyes on me. Hands to yourself, young man." The students visibly rippled as they diverted their gaze from Brett to their coach. "Ah, excuse me for interrupting, Coach Brett, but I see some behavior here that is not acceptable. You know who I'm talking about, and I don't want to see that again! Got it?" boomed Alex.

Rattled, Brett attempted to pick up the pace again, explaining more about the communication activity. Throwing at different levels would serve as a motor activity for the youngsters today. They would help each other perform the correct throwing pattern, while challenging themselves by using balls of various sizes thrown from partner to partner at different distances, through hoops, or into baskets. Increasing levels of difficulty would be encouraged, and each student would peer-coach a partner to help all reach greater competency from individual starting strengths.

Alex moved in shepherding several students to the field. "You two, over here. You use this ball and be the thrower. You catch. Same for you two. And you as well. Maintain positions until I can see that you're all standing and moving properly. Feet here. Ball this way. Release only after a step." Alex was now coaching several of the more skilled students. Brett frowned and thought, "I just can't get it across. Alex insists upon telling them every element of movement instead of letting the students construct their own understanding. As a result, everyone is doing the same thing, even though many are more advanced and some need to start at an earlier developmental place."

Frustration for Brett was mounting. Team teaching was becoming the nightmare he feared. None of the students were getting quality physical education. "Before I teamed up with Alex, at least 50 percent of the school's children were experiencing a more cohesive, integrated, and meaningful program," Brett thought.

"It's time for another decision," concluded Brett. "Better for me to go it alone again than to constantly be upset about having to do all the planning *and* implementation. All Alex is doing is putting students into time-out or coaching the elite athletes."

As the new teacher mulled over apparent options, Alex strode over whispering, "I've got news for you today, good buddy. You're about to get an award from Principal Chris—but you never heard it from these lips."

Brett was startled and asked, "Why would I get an award after being here for just three months?" Alex explained, "You remember. I told you Chris is into that 'learning community' thing. Well, everyone knows you are being an innovator out here. Even the parents are talking and writing complimentary notes about it. And they all know we're collaborating daily—even team teaching. Why you're mentoring an experienced teacher while I mentor you. So, you're going to get the Alachua Elementary School Colearner of the Month award for modeling such exemplary attitudes and behaviors. Congratulations, partner."

Brett straightened and silently questioned, "How am I going to pull out of team teaching when there is an award on the way for being collaborative?" Alex interrupted his thoughts. "By the way, I sure miss some of my favorite activities like 'kickball,' 'hug tag,' and 'slimy snake chain' where the kids roll all over each other. Since we're being collaborative, couldn't we put some of my favorite ones in there too?"

Following the fall festival, Brett again mused about recent events. "Maybe Alex should have gone as a dinosaur," thought Brett while pondering the goblin and ghost events. "Then again, Alex probably felt that I should have dressed as a traitor since I've asked to return to our original schedules and forget the team teaching." Brett's mind was churning again: "Surely Alex understands. There's no way we could pretend that what we were doing was team teaching. It was me carrying the load and Alex yelling at students for not being fast, talented, or tough enough." Brett shivered in the fall dampness and thought, "I almost lost it with the 'bunch of wimpettes who can't do a real push-up' remark during last month's fitness testing. In fact, I still cannot believe that I'm losing so much time to fitness testing when it makes so little sense to me and seems to take away so much of our learning time."

Brett did not hear Alex enter the office and was startled when the door slammed in the cold November wind. "Settle down, kid. Take it easy," said Alex. "Anyone ever tell you to lighten up?"

Brett laughed nervously saying, "You, and my guardian, and just about every teacher I've ever had. I know I'm too intense, but I just want to help change physical education so that children will turn on to physical activity and become more skillful and fit, and so that physical educators will receive more respect. Does that sound ridiculous to you?"

Alex paused and then pounced: "What do you think I've been doing these past 15 years, Coach? I've given the best years of my life to rug rats who crawl in and out of here without a clue. At least before, we could scare them into shape. Now, they won't listen or follow orders, and we can't even touch them without losing our jobs. What makes you think you're so much more committed or giving than I am? We share similar schedules and responsibilities, but I get the sense you don't approve of me or my program. In fact, I don't think you've considered a thing that I do worth squat. Tell me, Brett, what gives you that right?"

Later, Brett was grateful that he planned time with Alex in the field. It was time to pull it together and make some decisions. "I could just break my contract and quit today; or I could apologize and begin looking for the best of Alex's program while ignoring everything else; or we could just use separate courts, fields, and rooms during classes to keep out of each other's way," thought the frustrated teacher. More ideas began flowing: "I could wait until transfers are possible in the spring, or try for one of those new energy transfers to help the district and community cut down on fuel costs. What to do?"

The phone roused Brett to attention. "Hello. Dr. Nufau! I can't believe it's you. I never thought I would say this but, wow, do I miss you. I'm having quite a time here with Coach Winslow. In fact, it's hard to believe that she graduated from the same program. I really could use your support."

The former university supervisor responded quickly, "Well that's perfect, Brett, because we're thinking of ways to provide greater levels of support for our beginning teachers while generating additional hands-on experience for our interns. We're calling it the "Interactive Induction and Internship Program" and we would love for you to be a part of it. It would mean working with me as a cooperating teacher, along with two interns. You'd be modeling and expecting exemplary practice as you did within our previous program. You could continue learning with the interns as they learn with you, and I would be there regularly to provide ongoing support for all of you."

The professor continued enthusiastically, "The other great thing about this program is that it should increase your status at the school. Since physical educators often feel marginalized—especially as we begin our careers, this could offer powerful support for you from the faculty and administrators. What do you think, Brett? Would you be interested? If so, I can call Christine, your principal, for approval." Brett sighed with relief, thinking, "What an out! Maybe Alex will finally realize that I'm not a fool. I'm just a woman like her who cares about kids."

Name   Date

Preparing for Learning & Teaching

1. What is the critical issue in this case?

2. How does an elementary physical education teacher generate professional respect from colleagues who frequently marginalize the subject (e.g., refer to physical educators as "Coach" rather than "teacher")?

3. What are Alex's versus Brett's values regarding developmentally appropriate physical education? Could there be others? Explain.

4. What does a recent graduate who deeply believes in strategies and content that reflect the best practice according to today's standards do in the face of experienced teachers who mock their training?

5. What is a teacher's responsibility relative to liability (safety issues) and activity choices (e.g., relays and dodgeball)?

6. Regarding a learning community, Alex is "talking the talk," but what is "walking the walk"? What are the components of a true learning community?

7. Is there a place for conflicting values in elementary physical education? Is it better to share the same values for consistency and effective collaboration, or is it better to have different values so students can experience diverse ways of being and doing in the physical education context?

8. How can a beginning teacher change existing patterns of social segregation in a school (e.g., gender, race, and disability)? Is giving students choices about teammates helpful or harmful in a highly segregated setting?

9. Is there a role for competitive games in elementary physical education? What might be the impacts of such games on students, cooperation, and social responsibility levels?

10. What do you do with highly skilled students? How do you teach unskilled students without punishing or boring the skilled students?

11. When coteaching, what would you do if you saw undesirable behaviors, attitudes, values, or activities reflected by the other teacher?

12. What do you do when your colleague uses inappropriate language to describe you, students, or other colleagues (e.g., "wimps," "buns of steel," and "jocks")?

13. Can a new teacher refuse additional administrative responsibilities assigned by the principal? Or negotiate a compromise?

14. Is "you do your thing and I'll do mine" a good solution where colleagues have different values?

15. What attitudes and shared responsibilities would help make team teaching more effective?

16. How can you negotiate equipment and space with colleagues? What creative ways would help you generate additional equipment?

17. Are developing better communication skills and learning how to give specific feedback about performance to others appropriate learning objectives in elementary physical education?

18. What are the advantages and disadvantages of being videotaped during physical education classes? Would being featured during the principal's morning televised "welcome" be helpful to a physical education program?

19. What other strategies can you think of to enhance the attitudes of students, teachers, parents, communities, and administrators toward your physical education program?

20. In the throwing activity described during Brett's teaching, what developmentally appropriate strategies can you identify? How do Alex's strategies differ from Brett's?

21. In light of our diverse school populations (religion, culture, gender, ethnicity, etc.), how should a teacher examine issues involving physical contact between teachers and students, students and students, or students and others? Do activities like "hug tag" and "slinky snake chain" belong in an elementary physical education program?

22. Is there a role for fitness testing in elementary physical education? What are the assumptions and values such testing implies? Are these realistic? Are there other activities that would be a more effective response to these goals and values?

23. How do you handle a colleague's anger if she feels your values and curriculum content make her look bad?

24. Brett analyzed several options to deal with her problems with Alex, from going along to complete separation. Examine these options relative to advantages and disadvantages, and generate additional options that may be equally good or better.

25. What are the pros and cons of Brett participating with Dr. Nufau in the Interactive Induction and Internship Program?

26. Were you surprised that Alex, Brett, and Chris were all females? Examine your assumptions about gender (e.g., power, experience, coaches, administrators, beginners, athletes, language, dress, etc.). Would this case change for you if the characters' genders were different, and if so, how?

Traveling Teacher

Sandra A. Stroot

Carol Jones

Christine Bell

Case 12

O h what a beautiful morning," Sylvia Moreno was singing to herself as she drove to school and thought how lucky for her that the weather was holding so that she could finish her orienteering unit. This is the first year Sylvia has tried this unit, and the teachers and students at Maple have cooperated wholeheartedly. The curriculum director had encouraged the teachers to show initiative in integrating other subject materials into the curriculum. This was Sylvia's first effort to combine geography, math, and physical education. It took a lot of extra time and effort to plan with the other teachers. But, so far, it has been worth it.

Sylvia finally arrived at Maple Elementary School. At Maple, Sylvia taught all of the students from kindergarten through sixth grade. She was also assigned to teach some of the students at Elmhurst Elementary; however, Elmhurst did not have a gymnasium. Sylvia went to Harrison two afternoons per week to teach students who were bused from Elmhurst. It was very difficult to keep track of everything that was going on at the different school sites, especially at Harrison. Sylvia felt as though she was a viable part of Maple Elementary, but since she was only at Harrison two afternoons a week, she was not able to spend enough time to really know the school, the teachers, or the students. Communication was a problem because she did not usually get

> Sylvia was so tired of hauling all of this equipment. Maybe she would forego all that and just plan simple lessons for the Elmhurst students. She knew it would not be fair to the students, but she was feeling very frustrated.

her messages until the day she arrived. It was often too late to attend to the issues that arose. The contexts were also different at the two schools—students at Maple were from the middle and upper classes, while the students at Harrison were from a lower socioeconomic background.

Sylvia snapped out of her daydream as another teacher walked into the room. "Glad to see you here today, Sylvia. We've been working all week on our map reading," said Janie Jones, as she popped her head around the corner. Janie was one of the fifth-grade teachers at Maple Elementary School. "All I've heard from the students is, 'When do we have gym? When do we have gym?' They really are looking forward to your class!"

"Thanks, Janie. To tell the truth, so am I!"

As quickly as she popped her head in the door, Janie was gone to greet her students.

Sylvia stopped in the teachers' lounge for a cup of coffee. Jeff and Manuel, the other two fifth-grade teachers, were animatedly talking over some papers. They looked over and saw Sylvia coming into the room.

"Sylvia, come over here so we can show you what we've been doing with our classes this week. I think the students are more than ready for your orienteering challenge now!"

As Sylvia walked toward them, both Manuel and Jeff had big smiles on their faces. Jeff placed stacks of elaborately colored maps of countries, states, and counties in front of her. "Feast your eyes!" he said.

The students had drawn maps of the United States, their state and county, and detailed overhead views of Maple School and the adjacent park. Their maps were intricate. They contained buildings, trees, marked and measured distances, and extensive legends.

Sylvia was amazed by the quality of the students' work. "Very impressive, Jeff!"

"Yes! This challenge has really motivated my group," Jeff said. "Even Adam, who is the last to get interested in almost any task, can hardly wait to see if he can find his way through the course you are setting for them. Look at *his* map!" Jeff lifted a beautifully drawn map from the stack. It was so nicely designed, it looked almost professional.

"I didn't know Adam had that kind of ability!"

"That is the point," said Jeff. "Neither did anyone else! The other students have been just as excited, but this is the first project I've tried that has really brought Adam around. He has never been any trouble, but usually he just sits in class and stares out the window. None of my attempts to interest him seemed to work. But, look at this project—he was so excited he wanted to work on it all day long."

Manuel said, "The cooperative learning teams you formed in physical education have really helped my students work together. They seriously accepted the challenge you provided them—to prepare to follow a complex course on the school and park site. I'm sure they will enjoy finding their way through the course using their own maps. I think this activity has been so effective we should consider using this idea for a field day. Perhaps we should invite the parents to be on a team too!"

"Good idea, Manuel," said a voice from behind. Just entering the teachers' lounge was Erika Simmons, the principal. "Perhaps we can have the fourth and fifth grades participate in orienteering challenges, while the primary grades play cooperative games. What do you think, Sylvia? Would that work?"

"It would work for me if the teachers are interested. Can we talk more a bit later? I have to set up for my classes."

"Of course," said Erika. "Keep up the good work!"

Sylvia hurried to the gym to get equipment ready for the first class. The first two classes of third graders would be indoors. Today they would continue to create their own games. During the two previous classes, the students had learned games that had been designed by last year's third-grade students. In addition, they had learned how to design a game by working in groups of four. Each group had determined a name, boundaries, needed equipment, and an object, strategies, player responsibilities, and rules for playing a new game. The students summarized these on a written game form. Sylvia had instructed the students to make their games unique—unlike any other that they may have played. She looked over the game forms each group had turned in and recalled how animated the students were while refining their game during the previous lesson.

As the first class entered the gym that morning Sylvia sensed their excitement to begin. Once warm-up exercises were completed she called each group over, gave them their game forms, and directed them to gather their equipment from the sideline wall. Sylvia reminded them to review the written game forms to familiarize themselves with the object and rules of the games. She encouraged the groups to modify and revise the games as necessary once they had given them a trial run. While the students worked, Sylvia monitored the groups to determine if every student was included in the activity. She always made sure that the students with developmental challenges were being included and accepted by their classmates. Mike and Chelsie were in this class and sometimes needed special attention. Sylvia could see that Mike, a student with Down's Syndrome, was having a great time with his group as they rode their scooter boards and pushed the cageball toward the goal. At the other end of the gym she saw that Chelsie was not faring as well. She was sitting by the wall as the other students in the group took turns riding the hoppity-hop around the bases and shooting baskets.

Sylvia approached the group and Meghan met her as she reached their game boundaries. "Mrs. Sloan, Chelsie won't take a turn on the hoppity-hop!" Meghan said.

"Did anyone offer to help Chelsie with the hoppity-hop?" Sylvia asked.

All the group members shook their heads no. Meghan and Steve ran to Chelsie, holding her hand as they walked toward the hoppity-hop. Meghan said, "Come on, Chelsie, Steve and I will help you ride the hoppity-hop. Just sit down on it and jump with your legs as you bounce on it."

Steve said, "I was afraid to ride it at first too, but now I love it! I'll hold onto you so you'll feel safe."

Sylvia was delighted to see the group react as they did when she asked about helping Chelsie. She thought how nice it would be if all problems could be solved so easily. She complimented the group for using caring and sharing behaviors and walked over to observe and interact with two other groups.

It was soon time to put the equipment away and have the students return to their squads. The students were a big help, as Sylvia gave them specific responsibilities for the equipment. She knew the students at Maple well and felt as though they could handle these additional responsibilities.

The next third-grade class was as anxious to try their newly created games as had been the first. They had to set up the equipment before beginning, so Sylvia hustled them to hurry. They accomplished their set-up quickly and were soon engaged both physically and mentally. Sylvia was proud of her students' success in demonstrating behaviors that reflected responsibility and caring. Time flew by, and once again she was prompting the students to put the equipment back in the boxes. Sylvia pushed the boxes into the corner so she could get them quickly later. Thank goodness the teachers were on time!

After dismissing the third-grade class, Sylvia quickly pulled out the compasses, maps, clipboards, and pencils so she would be ready for the next two classes of fifth-grade students. Jeff Spicer walked his class to the door of the gym and said, "Well, here's the world's most excited class, Mrs. Moreno. They can't wait to begin your orienteering course this morning!"

With that, all of the students hurried to get into their groups. The students sat patiently as Sylvia explained how they would work in their assigned teams to find each location in the course. Each student had been previously assigned roles on their teams. One student would be the director and would help to organize and explain. Another had the role of equipment manager, responsible for compasses, clipboards, maps, and pencils. A third student would be the recorder and serve as the score-keeper/secretary, and the final group member would be the encourager and help by giving positive comments. The students gathered in their groups, and the class headed outside. They moved quickly to their starting points and began counting paces to the first marker on the course. Once they reached their first marker they read the directions posted on the tree and proceeded to the next point. The groups worked well together and laughed as they made their way around the course. Sylvia was surprised to see that Adam's group had chosen him as the director. Perhaps it was because of his outstanding map! As Sylvia watched the teams, she thought how glad she was that the staff had been receptive to the idea of integrating their curricula so the students could have this fun and unique learning experience.

Before Sylvia knew it, the end of class arrived and Mr. Spicer met them as the group walked toward the gym. "Well how was the orienteering?" he asked the class. The students answers were single-word exclamations like *awesome, great, outstanding, confusing, different,* and *fun!*

Manuel Ortega's class was the next to arrive. They, too, were impatient to begin the orienteering course. The students gathered in their groups of four and readied their equipment. Sylvia led them outside to explain how they would proceed through the course. When Sylvia asked if there were any questions, Nancy raised her hand and said, "Jason isn't here today so we are missing one team member." Just then Mr. Ortega ran to join the group, saying that he wanted to stay with the class today. Nancy said excitedly, "You can take Jason's place in our group, Mr. Ortega!" In no time at all, the groups completed the course and it was time to gather the equipment and go inside.

Sylvia knew she had to hurry to get to Harrison Elementary, so as soon as the students were gone, she ran to the gymnasium to quickly collect the equipment used at Maple, load it into her truck, and take to Harrison for her afternoon classes. She wished that Harrison had its own equipment so that she didn't have to take all of this with her! It took about ten minutes to load the third-grade equipment into the truck and then she had to get the equipment for orienteering. Before she locked the office door and headed toward the exits, she took a moment to review her afternoon schedule:

12:30–12:50	Playground duty at Elmhurst
12:50	Drive to Harrison and unload equipment
1:05–1:40	Third-grade creative games (at Harrison)
1:40–2:15	Third-grade creative games (at Harrison)
2:15	Drive to park for orienteering
2:20–2:55	Fifth-grade orienteering course (at park)
2:55–3:30	Fifth-grade orienteering course (at park)

It took two trips to get all of the orienteering markers, clipboards, and the remainder of the equipment into the truck, then Sylvia locked her office door and headed toward the exit.

Just then Kyle came running into the gym and said, "Mrs. Moreno, can I please use the air pump for our soccer ball? It's too flat to kick."

Sylvia was tempted to say no, but she knew how much the students enjoyed playing soccer at recess. She turned around and said "Sure Kyle, but hurry or I'll be late for my duty at Elmhurst." If she didn't always have rush to Harrison, it would be a lot easier to help students with their daily challenges!

When Kyle finished, Sylvia hurried to get into her truck. She had exactly ten minutes before her recess duty started at Elmhurst. As she drove, she ate a banana and a pack of peanut butter and cheese crackers for lunch. Maybe someday she could have a real lunch hour!

The students were happy to see Sylvia arrive at Elmhurst since her presence on the playground reminded them that they would have physical education class that afternoon. Recess duty was uneventful, but Sylvia was happy to see Mrs. Clawson come to relieve her so she could run inside to check her mailbox before heading to Harrison.

Pat Hanson, Elmhurst's principal, met her at the office door and said, "It's good to see you, Sylvia. Were you able to set up the orienteering course at the park?"

Sylvia answered, "Yes, and it should work just fine. I just wish we could have a field available here at Elmhurst like the one we have at Maple. I hope the bus driver remembers to bring the last two classes to the park instead of to Harrison. I guess I had better remind her when she brings the first class. I'd better hurry so I can get to Harrison and unload all of the equipment for the third-grade classes. See you at the end of the day."

Sylvia arrived at Harrison and propped the gym door open so she could carry the equipment inside. Harrison was always more crowded than Maple because the gym was also the lunchroom at Harrison, and there were tables lining the walls. As Sylvia looked inside she saw pipes, boards, boxes of hardware, and huge treated lumber posts scattered around the floor. Harrison's new playground apparatus had finally arrived, but why was it all over the gym floor? How was Sylvia supposed to have class?

She finished carrying all of the equipment inside and saw Keith, Harrison's custodian walking toward her. "This is certainly a surprise! When did this get here?" Sylvia asked. Keith patted her on the shoulder and said, "It has been here for a few days, but we didn't have anywhere else to put it. Maybe you can work around it. You're good at being flexible." Sylvia responded, "I don't think I can, Keith. This is a real safety problem today. We are in the middle of a creative games unit. We'll have to move these building supplies. Can you start moving them? I'll set up the equipment as we get the space cleared." Sylvia was frustrated with the lack of communication from the Harrison administrator. She did not like these surprises. She planned so thoroughly to make sure the students had quality learning experiences, then she spent her time fighting for teaching space.

She ran to unlock the storage room door and set her briefcase inside as Keith reluctantly began pushing the posts and pipes closer to the wall. Sylvia quickly set up the equipment for the third-grade classes and then began to help him. "Wow, is this stuff heavy!" she thought. Even though everything was up against the walls, she carried cones from her truck to create new boundaries so the third graders wouldn't get hurt as they worked on designing their games. Speaking of third graders, they were to arrive any minute! Sylvia called a quick "thank you" to Keith as she ran out of the gym door.

Sylvia hurried upstairs to meet the students as they arrived by bus from Elmhurst. They were pretty rowdy from the bus ride so she kept them outside the door until they calmed down. They walked to the gym and Sylvia cautioned the students to stay within the new boundaries as she sent them to their warm-up stations. Once the station activities were completed, they returned to squads where Sylvia distributed their game forms and reminded them to review the rules and object of their games as she had earlier that day for the Maple students. The students gathered their equipment from the side wall and began playing their games.

The class went quickly, and soon it was time to put the equipment away and have the students return to squads. She evaluated their performance as a class and then dismissed the squads individually to form a line. The class walked upstairs to meet the bus, but it wasn't there yet. Sylvia let those students who wanted to get a drink of water go downstairs to the drinking fountain while the rest waited on the stairs for the bus to arrive. Finally after a ten-minute wait the bus came around the corner. As Sylvia chatted with the bus driver, she discovered that Mrs. Compton's class was late getting to the bus at Elmhurst, so that's why they were late. It seems that they had a guest speaker who didn't finish on time. These problems are always more critical when students and teachers have to travel to the gym.

The class moved quickly to the gym and Sylvia said, "Since we are already fifteen minutes late we will do a couple of exercises in our groups instead of rotating stations today." After they had finished, Sylvia distributed the game forms so that the groups could get their equipment and set up their games. The class was able to get on task quickly. All of the groups worked effectively since they were accustomed to working in groups in Mrs. Compton's classroom. Sylvia moved from group to group reminding each to review their game forms, in particular, the object and the rules. When class was almost over, the equipment was returned to the side wall, and the class discussed their ability to work cooperatively to complete their game.

Jimmy raised his hand and said, "How can class be over already?" Sylvia reminded him that the class had arrived late; but hopefully next week they would have their full class time. As she led the students to board the bus, Sylvia reminded the bus driver to deliver the next two classes to the park so they could do orienteering. Sylvia grabbed the necessary equipment, first-aid box, and student emergency cards before heading to her truck. She planned to drive to the park to meet the students. She was excited to try the integration theme with the orientation unit at Elmhurst. Students from lower socioeconomic backgrounds were not generally exposed to this kind of experience. Elmhurst was located in a poorer section of the city, and the parks there were not nearly as big as the one they would be using for orienteering.

As she reached the park Sylvia noticed the city tractors mowing the grass. She thought, "Why now? Why couldn't they have mowed yesterday?"

Sylvia hurried from the truck, carrying the compasses, maps, clipboards, pencils, and first-aid box. She placed the equipment on the bench by the ball diamond and saw the bus turning the corner. As the students got off the bus they ran toward the ball diamond. Sylvia called to them to meet her by the bench and soon organized them into orienteering groups.

Marcus raised his hand and said, "How can we do our orienteering with those tractors in the way?"

Sylvia explained to Marcus and the rest of the class that everyone would have to be flexible and use only half of the course until the men were finished mowing. After some mumbling and groaning, the groups proceeded to the beginning of the course. The students enjoyed working together even though Sylvia had to talk loudly over the roar of the mowers.

The class was over before the mowing was completed so Sylvia promised the students that they would do the complete course the following day. They gathered at the bench and the bus pulled up to the curb to take them back to Elmhurst. Sylvia waved goodbye as the bus pulled away. She had about five minutes before the next class should arrive, so she took time to organize the clipboards and orienteering markers. Sylvia sat on the bench and waited for Mrs. Brown's class.

After more than ten minutes, she began to wonder what the problem was this time. Could it be another guest speaker, or were the students late in returning from instrumental class, or were they just so noisy that they couldn't get organized on time? Another ten minutes passed and still no class! Just then the bus turned the corner, but it was empty! As the bus stopped, she ran to the door and the driver said, "Sorry, Sylvia, Mrs. Brown's class went on a field trip this afternoon and forgot to tell us! You may as well clean up your equipment and head back to Harrison."

Sylvia had worked hard to prepare for the orienteering course. The students would be disappointed also. Perhaps she could make up the course next class, but that would put the group another week behind the other fifth-grade classes. It would also mean carrying all of the equipment back and forth from Harrison again. As she gathered the equipment, Sylvia became increasingly upset. She wondered how Mrs. Brown could have forgotten something so important? She wouldn't dream of taking a field trip without notifying the classroom teacher in advance. She was so tired of hauling all of this equipment. Maybe she would forego all that and just plan simple lessons for the Elmhurst students. She knew it would not be fair to the students, but she was feeling very frustrated.

It was amazing how Sylvia could accomplish so much more at Maple, even something as complex as the integrated units. The communication factor was so important, and it just did not occur at Harrison. How could she convince the teachers it was necessary?

Too bad the school district can't hire more physical education teachers so Sylvia could teach full-time at Maple and not have to deal with the situation. If more teachers can't be hired, why don't they bus the Elmhurst students to Maple, where the equipment is available and the facilities are so much better? Life as a teacher would be far less complicated and stressful if the district would make a couple of reasonable changes. As Sylvia pondered these questions, she soon realized that she was back at Harrison and had to clean up the equipment from the third-grade classes and put it back in the truck for classes at Maple tomorrow morning. Maybe she should speak to her building principals. What would she say to convince them?

It had been a long day, and Sylvia was anxious to go home.

Name   Date

Preparing for Learning & Teaching

1. What is the critical issue in this case?

2. In what ways was the integrated project serving as a motivational vehicle for those involved? Can you think of other areas that could be developed as an integrated unit with classroom teachers and physical education teachers?

3. What suggestions could you offer to Sylvia to help open the lines of communication between Maple, Elmhurst, and Harrison Elementary Schools? How could she initiate the process?

4. How can you tell that Sylvia really cares about her students as individuals? What examples can you site? What values are included in her teaching?

5. Why did it seem so easy to marginalize physical education? Was Sylvia so flexible that the administrators, teaching staff, and custodians felt like they could take advantage of her and not respect her as a professional with the need to teach in a safe and appropriate area?

6. What are the major roadblocks that Sylvia faces in this scenario?

7. What would a teacher who was less committed to presenting quality and developmentally appropriate lessons have done when faced with the same struggles in and/or roadblocks to his/her teaching?

8. If Sylvia had not been so flexible and instead had demanded that she have equipment in each building, a safe and appropriate area in which to teach, and a more realistic schedule, how might this have affected her situation?

9. How could Sylvia approach the administration about the unrealistic expectations of trying to teach the course without equipment and an appropriate teaching area? What if the administration didn't hear her? What should be her next course of action?

10. As a beginning teacher who receives a similar teaching assignment, what would you do differently than Sylvia?

Inclusion II

Samuel Hodge

John Blaine

Case 13

My name is Jane White and I am a veteran physical education teacher. A number of years ago I attended a large flagship university in the Midwest while pursuing an undergraduate degree in teaching. At that time I considered myself an active physical education major. Moreover, while attending college I worked within the recreation department's intramural program, played on a couple of the softball and basketball league teams, and volunteered to coach volleyball at a nearby high school. Those experiences further cemented my belief that teaching physical education was an excellent career choice. My initial desire was to teach physical education at the high school level. However, unsuccessful at securing a position at that level (limited jobs were available at the secondary level during the time I was pursuing a position), I eventually applied for and accepted a teaching position at a local elementary school. I've now been teaching physical education at Bluffton Elementary School for more than 15 years. After many years of teaching, I'm even more convinced that physical education is essential to enhance the development of elementary-age students. In addition to my regular teaching duties and responsibilities, I further serve the school community by coaching the local high school girls' varsity basketball and volleyball teams. In recent years, I've attended evening classes at

Now several of the students without disabilities (including Billy) were moving about, laughing, and being disruptive. I yelled "FREEZE." They stopped—but not Burton. I turned as Billy was now copying Burton's behavior and Burton was grinning as he yelled, "I'm Burrnen, I wov." The class was laughing hysterically. Meltdown had occurred!

the university for graduate credit toward a master's degree in physical education. Additionally, during the spring and summer months I volunteer as a coach for our regional Special Olympics organization.

Bluffton Elementary School is 1 of 12 public school buildings in the Portofino public school system located in a rapidly developing suburban area. I like living in this growing community with my husband. He also teaches and coaches in this school district. Our community is comprised predominantly of middle-class white Americans. However, in recent years families representing other ethnic/cultural groups have moved into our community. For example, a small percentage of African-American and Asian-American families now reside in the community. Some of their children attend Bluffton Elementary.

Typically, as a result of a shortage of physical education teachers in the school district and an ever-increasing student enrollment, physical education teachers (including myself) must travel daily from one school site to another to teach at two or more schools. And unfortunately, I feel that the physical education programs within the district are limited, in that our classes meet for only one 55-minute period each week at each school site. On the other hand, however, schools in the district are very well equipped with multipurpose rooms, large spacious gymnasiums, excellent indoor and outdoor facilities for traditional and nontraditional activities, and supplies.

The first day of the new school year began with a typical sunny, yet slightly cool, August morning. As the morning sun warmed the fresh air and the many excited students arrived for school, teachers began to familiarize themselves with new student faces and new and returning students began to familiarize themselves with their new class assignments. It seemed as if this bright, clear morning encouraged everyone to look forward to the coming school year with hopeful anticipation. I had spent the previous week refurbishing and cleaning equipment, and preparing to meet the excited smiles of both new and returning students. The school's janitor had cleaned and polished the gymnasium floor, and I wasted no time diligently marking home bases for the students.

With the start of a new school year, I was prepared to use my bag of tricks and management strategies to control student behavior and also ensure high levels of active learning time—or as Dr. Hard, my professor at the university, called it, "academic learning time" (ALT). First, I planned to convey to the students my class expectations within the context of rules and routines. I knew that it would be easy to remind the returning students of the previous year's guidelines for appropriate behavior, expectations, and procedures. For those students new to the school, I would provide clear and specific explanations and practice opportunities so they could understand their individual and collective responsibilities. I was aware that this year's student population was more diverse than in prior years. I was confident that my classes would soon reflect good class management and high levels of ALT.

My assumptions rang true that first school day, as many of the returning students could readily recall the rules and routines learned during the previous school year. Still, I felt that it was important to provide opportunities in each period to practice some of the rules and routines that would be used throughout the year. Some students needed a few prompts regarding class expectations. Most of them, however, could clearly articulate the previously established rules and routines, so little time was spent reteaching these concepts. Much to my delight and surprise, several of the new students were already picking up the concepts. Toward the day's end, I was able to begin teaching fundamental locomotor skills without spending much time reviewing rules and routines. Yes, the first day of the new school year was off to a great start!

While driving to work the following day, I was still excited and confident that my classes would run as smoothly as they had on the previous day. Mrs. Wilson's class of kindergarten students entered the gymnasium for their first day of physical education, and I instructed them on finding self-space. Mrs. Wilson called me over to advise me that two students with disabilities would be included in this group. I couldn't stop to talk with her about it further because the students were already in the gymnasium awaiting my instructions. I wasn't really concerned about having students with disabilities in my physical education classes since I had worked with them before on several occasions.

As the students entered, most of them sat three to four feet from their classmates, and many of them sat in a cross-legged manner. I noticed that four students had not yet located a space to sit. I reiterated the original direction, and one little girl, who was wearing a pretty purple matching outfit, quickly stopped talking and located a self-space. (This child was new to the school, and I later learned that her name was Cheryl.) Further, I noticed that she held her right arm drawn up in a flexed position close to her body and walked with a limp on that same side. I guessed that she must have had cerebral palsy but later learned that her hemiplegia (paralysis affecting one side) was due to a car accident resulting in a traumatic brain injury. Cheryl functioned motorically at a level behind her peers, but she always seemed to put forth her best effort. Important to class management, however, was that she responded immediately to my directions, and it seemed that Cheryl would not present any unusual disciplinary concerns.

I turned my attention to the other students who had found their self-spaces and loudly praised them (hoping those three students who had not yet properly responded would do so). Although this was one of the behavioral strategies we had discussed in one of my graduate courses, it did not appear to be working with these three students. One of the off-task students was a short, stocky boy, who looked as if he had Down's syndrome and probably moderate-to-severe mental retardation. I had worked with many children with Down's syndrome in previous years and could readily recognize the characteristics. "Well, these must be the two students that Mrs. Wilson had mentioned earlier," I thought to myself. I realized that I needed to move quickly since the three off-task students were still not responding to my prompting. I feared losing control of those students who were on-task and hoped their patience would hold up. I darted across the gym floor toward the stocky little boy. He was bumping and sliding along the gym wall. I stepped in front of him placing my hands on his right shoulder, bending down to make eye contact and asked, "What's your name?"

He responded, "Burrrnn."

"I did not understand; say that again," I prompted.

"Burrnnen," he replied again in a louder, impatient voice, yet I still did not understand.

"His name is Burton," explained a classmate sitting close by.

Although Burton still needed my attention, I could not neglect the whole class and risk total "behavioral control meltdown," which could occur at any moment. I quickly led Burton to the nearest open space and helped him sit with his legs crossed. He seemed to like doing what he now realized the other students were doing, so I praised him and the whole class for sitting quietly with their legs crossed.

I sprinted over toward the other two off-task students. They were interlocked in a human pile on the floor wrestling, rolling, kicking, laughing, and moaning in loud bursts. I pulled them apart, moving each child about four feet from the other, and demanded that they sit down! I again offered praise to reinforce those students who were still waiting but becoming distracted. One of the "wrestlers," an African-American student, seemed to be somewhat disoriented. I led him by his arm to a self-space and directed him to sit down. "Perhaps, this child has attention deficit disorder," I considered. Later, I learned that his name was Lamar and that he responded best to direct instructions. Billy, the second "wrestler," selected a space and sat down near Mindy. Billy seemed "typical," at least judging from how he looked. If only I had help!

I took a breath while taking a step backward to view the whole class and to gather my thoughts. I observed several of the initially on-task and in-place students starting to show clear signs of restlessness and decided to introduce my starting and stopping commands. As I attempted to explain how to "move" and "freeze" on command, several previously on-task students were now looking and laughing at Burton as he ran around in circles. (Cheryl and Lamar were still sitting quietly in place.) "Oh, no, if Burton has difficulty sitting still for just 10 seconds, how in the world will I ever get anything accomplished?" I worried. Now several of the students without disabilities (including Billy) were moving about, laughing, and being disruptive. I yelled "FREEZE." They stopped—but not Burton. I turned as Billy was now copying Burton's behavior and Burton was grinning as he yelled, "I'm Burrnen, I wov." The class was laughing hysterically. Meltdown had occurred!

An observer might think that I had no management skills or awareness of behavioral control strategies. I wondered how I would ever be able to manage such a diverse group of students so that learning could take place. My structured plans for management had fallen apart. I was able to reestablish control with the majority of the class but was not able to get Burton and Billy on-task. We spent the rest of the class practicing management strategies and never got to locomotor skills. I needed help!

(And I needed more information about Burton and Billy to be able to attend to each of their needs and interests.)

After class, Mrs. Wilson apprised me of the situation regarding the two students with disabilities (Cheryl and Burton). She felt that they could be included if we were provided the information from their IEPs (Individualized Education Programs) and the support of teacher aides, speech therapist, and the like. Mrs. Wilson would not speculate as to why Lamar did not have an IEP and was not receiving special programming. We agreed, however, that when given direct instructions, Lamar immediately responded with appropriate behavior. Upon further reflection, I decided that neither Cheryl nor Lamar would be cause for concern. Billy, although not considered disabled, was much more of a disciplinary concern. Mrs. Wilson apologized for not speaking with me sooner and suggested that I talk with Mr. Caldwell (the building principal), Mrs. Pitts (their special education teacher), and other IEP team members about Burton. "Who should I speak with about Billy?" I wondered.

I knew the school district was implementing a new program to comply with IDEA (Individuals with Disabilities Education Act) amendments and that the least restricted environment for some children with disabilities is the general physical education context. I support inclusion and its intended long-term benefits for children with and without disabilities. In fact, I have always disagreed with the separation that occurs as a result of students being labeled and stuffed into "special" classrooms. Some children with severe disabilities or who look different are mistreated, shown little respect, and become the target of unkind remarks from students and school staff.

I wondered why no support personnel (e.g., speech therapist or teacher aides) had accompanied those students with disabilities to my physical education class. Moreover, it now appeared that I would need to assist in developing these children's IEPs. What can I possibly learn from reviewing their IEPs? I also wondered who decides what child will have an IEP drafted. Should Lamar have an IEP? Should I call his parents and ask them about this matter? What if he does not have a disability? Could Lamar's behaviors be related to cultural differences and not any disabling condition? What about Billy? His misbehavior does not appear to be attributable to an identified disability or cultural differences. I have so many questions that need to be addressed. Exhausted after my second day of school, I felt confused and concerned.

Name   Date

Preparing for Learning & Teaching

1. What is the critical issue in this case?

2. Who are the characters in the case?

3. What role did the characters play in creating/solving these issues?

4. What are some of the suggested strategies you might use to address these issues?

5. How should inclusion be defined? Do you agree with this practice?

6. Although she may or may not be cognizant of them, what are some of the confounding issues that confront Ms. White? Can you think of other less obvious issues?

7. Should physical educators be required to be involved in the IEP of all students with special needs? Why or why not?

8. What are some of the specific elements that contributed to these issues?

9. Can you describe some of the legal mandates impacting students with special needs? How does this impact your class?

10. What are the related issues and questions raised by this case?

11. What strategies might you use to address these issues?

Urban Challenge

Shaun M. Wuthrich
Sandra A. Stroot

Case 14

Greg Owens closed the teachers' lounge door and sank heavily into the chair. Removing his glasses, Greg rubbed his eyes, exhaled, and as he replaced his glasses he glanced at a slip of paper with Quinton's home phone number. Once again, Quinton, a third grader, had been involved in a fight during physical education. When Mr. Owens had pulled the boys aside to discuss the situation, all he got was a wall of sullen silence. The other children who had witnessed the fight had told him that Travis had made a derogatory comment about one of Quinton's family members. Travis wouldn't admit to what he had said, and Quinton only lowered his head, looked at the ground, and had refused to speak.

Greg never remembered being this tired at the end of the day at his old school, Lakeview Elementary. Even though this was his fifth year of teaching, it was his first year at Washington Elementary. After graduation, Greg had moved back to his hometown, a small rural farming community, to teach. It was the type of town where everybody knew everybody, with only one post office, a drug store, a hardware store, a grocery store, a local cafe, and a few churches. In essence, the sidewalks rolled up at dark.

It was not to say things were perfect at Lakeview Elementary. The school and community had their share of children with learning difficulties and discipline problems. As a whole, the children were quiet,

Every Monday morning when Greg arrived at work, he had to clean up the playground from the previous weekend. The field and hardtop were littered with fast-food containers, beer cans, broken glass, and occasionally Greg would find objects that he was sure were drug paraphernalia.

calm, and obedient, and the parents and community had been support-ive of education and teachers. Even though Greg loved his hometown, his old school, and the children he worked with, he had felt bored and restless. It was a 60-mile drive to the closest movie theater or to a decent restaurant. He was excited, if not a little apprehensive, about living in the city where life was faster and more stimulating. Greg felt that the city would offer more opportunities for him socially and professionally.

After the first few months in the city, Greg found that he liked the excitement, although it had taken him a while to adjust to the noise. Not only was city life noisier but the activity of the city was reflected in the school and community where he worked. The children and the neighborhood were more animated, boisterous, and colorful. On some mornings, the noise on the playground was so deafening that one could actually hear the children several blocks away from the school.

Washington Elementary was a large inner-city school in a lower socioeconomic area. The school had a diverse population of approxi-mately 85 percent African-American and Hispanic, equally divided. The remaining 15 percent were mostly Caucasian from equally low socioeco-nomic backgrounds. Since most of the students were on free or reduced lunch, the school was classified as a Title One school. Class size was nego-tiated by the union and usually ranged from 20 to 25 in the primary grades and 25 to 30 in the intermediate grades.

Washington Elementary was a two-story, brick building with large floor-to-ceiling, single-pane windows. Many of the windows had been painted over. Even with the light-colored paint, the halls and stairwells seemed dark and dreary. Though recently painted, one could tell that the previous paint had not been scraped because it had that chipped tex-ture, not to mention that the colors didn't exactly match. Greg was sure this was due to the repeated vandalism that occurred at the school.

Greg was pulled from his trance as two other teachers walked out the door, chatting and laughing. He wondered how long it would be before he would be laughing at the end of the day again. Remembering he had told Quinton he would have to call his parents if another problem occurred, Greg picked up the phone receiver and dialed the number. As the phone was ringing, Greg hoped this would not be a rerun of a recent phone contact he had with another student's parent. When Greg had spoken with Lakishea's mother about fighting in physical education, she had sounded bitter, angry, and distrustful. Greg had gotten the distinct impression that she was an abandoned, single parent who did not want to be bothered with Lakishea's school behavior. The person answering the phone had never heard of Quinton—another wrong number. Greg would walk to the front office and check this number with the one on Quinton's office card.

Greg was also learning that many of the students did not have tele-phones at home, which made it difficult to contact their parents or guardians. The principal, Ms. Adams, had addressed this problem at one of the first faculty meetings by suggesting home visits. Greg had origi-nally dismissed this thought. How could he ever possibly meet with the parents of all 450 children he had in physical education? Now he wondered if Ms. Simmons, Quinton's classroom teacher, had made a visit to Quinton's home yet. If not, perhaps they could schedule a visit together.

Fighting during physical education was not the only problem Greg was experiencing. He struggled with many of the children. So much of his time was spent trying to get them to focus on the lesson that Greg felt he never got to teach. Today he'd had a tough time in several classes. He couldn't get his primary children to hold still long enough to answer questions. When Greg finally got the students focused, they had just called out the answers. Greg had worked repeatedly with them to get them to raise their hands and wait to be called on, rather than blurting out the answers. After Greg scolded the students, they would look down at the floor and quit responding to questions altogether.

Then there were the twins in a third-grade class who had wanted to sit on a mat during class. When Greg glanced over a few minutes later, they were fast asleep. He wondered if they might be sick. But when he saw them later during lunch, they seemed fine, laughing and chattering with their classmates. Greg noticed that sometimes they just didn't want to do anything, but at other times they were really excited about what was happening in physical education class. It just did not make much sense to him. He meant to ask about them but had been so busy it had slipped his mind.

After lunch, Greg had thought that he could get the fifth-grade students quickly grouped by giving them different-colored wristbands as they entered the gym. Ten different colors and thirty students in the class had worked out perfectly. As the students entered, they put on a wristband, chose the type of ball they wanted to use, and began to dribble in self-space. Greg used this management strategy because it gave him time to take care of any individual student concerns while the rest of the class was working on a task related to the daily activity. Next, Greg instructed the students to find other classmates with the same color of wristband. While maintaining self-space, two of the group members would match their dribbling to the third group member who acted as the group leader. When Greg called "time," each group would switch to a new leader. The lesson had been working well, so Greg was not overly concern when he noticed that some of the students had either traded colors or were wearing their wristband on another body part, such as an upper arm, thigh, or their head. Wearing the wristbands on their head was a potential health problem, however.

As Greg made a mental note to discuss this during closure, he heard Chaquise angrily shouting, "Don't be sooo stupid! Get rid of those things!" Sam, Jared, and Chaquise were arguing. Chaquise, a large, mature fifth grader, was glaring at them and had both fists clenched as though she was ready to punch.

During the first few weeks of school, Chaquise had been very quiet, but now she was becoming increasingly more argumentative and belligerent with the other students. Mr. Jackson, Chaquise's classroom teacher, was concerned about her and had brought the change to Greg's attention. However, this was the first time Chaquise had acted out in Greg's class. Earlier as the students were entering the gym, she had expressed her excitement about playing basketball. When the children saw Greg approaching, they immediately stopped arguing. Sam and Jared said they didn't feel well and wanted to sit out. Greg thought they might need to cool down so he agreed, saying, "Go ahead and sit on the stage for a few minutes. I'll come over in a moment and check on you."

After a few minutes, Greg went over to Sam and Jared. They said they felt fine now and wanted to go back into the activity. Greg let them go, noticing their red wristbands were still on the stage. He was so busy with other issues he just picked them up and put them in the wristband container. The boys seemed to know which group they were supposed to be in without them. Since they were back on task, Greg let the situation go. What a day!

Greg pulled Quinton's card from the file box and found he had the correct number, or at least the same one the office had. Greg decided to talk to Ms. Simmons about a home visit.

While walking upstairs to Ms. Simmons' classroom, Greg remembered the first time Quinton had gotten into trouble in his class. Quinton had lowered his head and refused to talk. Greg had demanded that he look at him, sternly raising his voice, "Young man, look at me when I'm talking to you!" When Quinton had not raised his head to look at him, Greg had resisted a strong desire to lift Quinton's chin. But, Quinton had stood there so rigid and distraught that Greg was afraid that if he touched him, Quinton would bolt like a caged animal. Greg had angrily thought to himself that Quinton was being rude, disrespectful, and evasive. As Greg entered the classroom, he asked, "Ms. Simmons, do you have a moment?"

The next day as the last bell rang, Greg locked the door to the P. E. office. He hurried to Mr. Vance in the guidance counselor's office. Greg wasn't tired today. His conversation with Ms. Simmons had been successful and enlightening. Ms. Simmons was concerned not only about Quinton's fighting, but about his reading as well. She had suggested that they go downstairs and enlist Mr. Vance's help. The three of them had talked until 5:30 P.M. and agreed to meet the next day and ride to school together. They not only discussed the situation with Quinton but Greg shared some of his other frustrations and concerns. It had been difficult at first to admit that he had problems, but once he got started an enormous weight had lifted.

One by one Greg recounted each situation. As for the phone call with Lakishea's mother, Mr. Vance had explained, "That lack of parent cooperation is not uncommon. Many parents from lower socioeconomic areas did not have positive or successful personal school experiences of their own; therefore, they are wary and distrustful of the so-called 'system.'"

Mr. Vance chuckled a bit when Greg told him about the kindergartners calling out the answers to his questions. He explained, "Sometimes when the students call out in class, they are trying to be involved in the only way they've been taught while growing up. We have a large population of Southern Baptists in this community. I belong to the Baptist church downtown, and you will find my church members participating through spontaneous responses during the entire service. When children from my church come into kindergarten, they have learned that it is appropriate to respond out loud, and need more time to adjust if you want them to raise their hand first. Just make sure you give them clear directions, and plenty of prompts, and they will learn what you expect in school. They are trying to participate in your class just like they have learned to participate in their church."

After Mr. Vance's explanation, Greg had to laugh at his naivete, realizing that his own religious experiences colored his expectations. He had grown up in a conservative Catholic church where if he had called out spontaneous responses during the service, he would probably have been asked to leave!

Mr. Vance explained that there could be many reasons for the twins falling asleep in class. When both parents work, the children cannot be left home alone and it is too expensive to pay a sitter. Sometimes the children go to work with their parents and may even wait in the car if necessary. This was the first time Greg had heard of this type of problem. Mr. Vance, however, promised he would check on the situation.

When Greg mentioned the episode with Chaquise, Sam, and Jared, Mr. Vance, who was aware of Chaquise's change in behavior, only questioned Greg about the color of the wristband each of the students had been assigned. Greg wondered why the color of the wristbands was of significance, but Mr. Vance changed the subject.

As it turned out, Quinton wasn't being rude or disrespectful when he refused to look at Greg. "Just the opposite," Mr. Vance explained. "In some families, neighborhoods, and cultures it is considered disrespectful to look a person of authority in the eye."

Ms. Simmons had grown up in the neighborhood and volunteered to drive. As the car turned out of the school parking lot, Greg noticed the vacated buildings surrounding the school, mostly abandoned factories and commercial buildings. There was a look of neglect. High fences with razor wire encircled most of the properties. Just driving through the neighborhood was depressing. No wonder the kids were angry and distrustful. How could a child become interested or excited about school if she had to live with the feeling of impending danger.

The neglected properties reminded Greg of Mondays. Every Monday morning when Greg arrived at work, he had to clean up the playground from the previous weekend. The field and hardtop were littered with fast food containers, beer cans, broken glass, and occasionally Greg would find objects that he was sure were drug paraphernalia. Sometimes Greg referred to the playground as the party zone.

"Well, I think this is the place." Ms. Simmons pulled the car into the driveway of one of the surrounding sandy brown block duplexes. They were in a federally subsidized area known as John Leslie. From the outside the duplexes appeared to be 2-bedroom/1-bath homes. Some of the buildings were in need of repair, and not a blade of grass grew in the small yards. Yet, some of the other homes had well-kept lawns, shrubs, and even flowers growing in containers and window boxes. Greg wondered who was responsible for maintaining the buildings and property.

As the three approached the door, Mr. Vance knocked. They could hear both the television and the radio playing inside. Mr. Vance knocked louder. The door cracked and a teenage girl peered out. Mr. Vance smiled and said, "Hi, I'm Mr. Vance, the guidance counselor at Washington Elementary. Is this Quinton William's house?"

The teenager nodded without a word.

"We were hoping to speak to Quinton's mother."

"She's not here," stated the teenager.

"Shantel, is that you?" interjected Ms. Simmons. "Remember me? I'm Ms. Simmons."

As the teenager visibly relaxed and nodded, Ms. Simmons continued, "Could we come in and perhaps talk with your grandmother?"

Shantel, Quinton's sister, closed the door. From the hallway the three educators could hear the clicking and clacking as several locks were being disengaged. Opening the door, Shantel turned and yelled, "Turn that thing off!" to a preschool-age boy.

As the three stepped into the apartment, Greg was amazed. He wasn't sure what he had expected. He hated to think it was some stereotypic image. The apartment, though small, was clean and orderly. The furnishings had a well-worn but comfortable look. The walls were covered with various family pictures and one could smell supper on the stove.

Shantel stated, "Mom is at work and grandma is at choir practice. What's Quint done now? He in trouble again?"

"No, I wouldn't say Quinton is in trouble, but he is having some problems. Where is your mother working now? I thought she worked at the textile plant." replied Ms. Simmons.

"She do," responded Shantel. "She works most evenin' over at that new Mexican restaurant, too."

Handing Shantel his school business card, Mr. Vance stated, "Well, when she gets in, please ask her to call either Ms. Simmons or myself at her earliest convenience."

As they turned to leave, Greg's eyes rested on another young child still in training pants doing serious justice to a peanut butter and jelly sandwich. Greg wondered if the toddler was Shantel's. "Dinner sure smells good," Greg commented.

As Ms. Simmons turned out of the entrance, Greg thought he spotted Chaquise on the corner. She was surrounded by several much older boys and girls, all similarly dressed. "Mr. Vance, isn't that Chaquise over there?" But before Mr. Vance could turn around in the seat, Ms. Simmons had guided the car onto the street. Glancing in the rearview mirror, Ms. Simmons quietly asked, "Do you think they are Crips?"

"Yes," replied Mr. Vance, equally as quiet.

Name   Date

Preparing for Learning & Teaching

1. What is the critical issue in this case?

2. What are some of the differences between Greg's rural background and his current urban setting?

3. Several situations occurred in Greg's class that he was not able to handle immediately. Can you describe some reasons why they may have occurred?

   ▪ Primary children calling out answers rather than raising their hands.

   ▪ Children looking down at the floor when scolded.

   ▪ The twins' inconsistent behavior—sleeping in class, chatting later at lunch.

   ▪ The scene between Chaquise, Sam, and Jared.

- Red wristbands left on the stage.

4. Describe the school environment. The surrounding neighborhood. How might this impact the students?

5. When visiting Quinton's house, what stereotype might Greg have inferred?

6. What are "Crips"?

7. If you found yourself in Greg's situation, how might you get more information about the lives of the children in your class?

8. What are the related issues and questions raised by this case?

9. What strategies might you use to address these issues?

Gender Equity

Susan K. Lynn

Kristie L. Walsdorf

Lori Nevin

Case 15

O NE, TWO, THREE, LOOK AT ME!" Cyndi Petrelli, the physical education teacher, yelled across the field as she made a circular motion overhead with her hand. The fourth-grade class stopped working and moved toward her. They knew the "round-up" hand motion was a signal to come in for group time.

Ms. Petrelli had been teaching physical education at Glennview Elementary since the school had opened ten years earlier. She felt strongly about teaching and the role of physical education. She had worked hard to establish and implement a well-rounded program of dance, gymnastics, sports and games, and fitness.

As the children came closer, some running, some trotting, others walking, Ms. Petrelli surveyed her students and thought, "What a great group of kids. Always on task and self-motivated, they really do an amazing job with child-centered indirect methods of instruction. So little class management with this group, I sometimes wonder if they really need me."

In fact, after their running exercise, only two students had to be redirected to what they were supposed to be doing. After greeting the class, Ms. Petrelli had instructed them to take one lap, get a partner, a glove, a ball, and practice their throwing and catching skills. The class had shot off like a rocket, cheering. It was a beautiful, clean, crisp fall day, perfect for working out in the field.

As David rose to demonstrate the overhand throwing pattern, Eddie and James started elbowing each other, giggling, and snickering. "Yeah, watch David, he throws just like a girl," singsonged James. Ms. Petrelli watched David's face fall as several classmates laughed.

Over the years Glennview had outgrown the school's facilities. With each year, Ms. Petrelli had to adjust to the increasing number of portables on the playground, as well as physical education instructional areas. Glennview's population was primarily middle class, with a typical ethnic balance. Many of the Glennview parents worked in professional and paraprofessional careers. Most of the students came from homes with two working parents.

About this time Eric, who was small for his age but very athletic, pretended to slide into home plate at Ms. Petrelli's feet, kicking up a cloud of grass and dirt. As she shook the grass and dust first from one foot and then the other, she gave Eric a mildly exasperated look. Eric rolled away laughing, knowing Ms. Petrelli wasn't really irritated even though she tried to act like she was. "Eric, that was uncalled for," called Calvin. Ms. Petrelli thought, "Calvin sounds just like me. Funny how some children can imitate so. Not just tone of voice, but facial expressions and body gestures also."

Calvin's asthma was much better this year. In second grade it had really flared up. Ms. Petrelli had made him a special helper that year. While the other children ran at the beginning of class, she had given Calvin the important job of delivering paperwork to the front office and checking her mailbox. Two years later, on his own initiative, Calvin still picked up her mail and placed it on her desk every morning.

As more children approached, Ms. Petrelli's eyes came to rest on Murphy. Murphy held one of the best one-mile times, boy or girl, for Glennview Elementary. When Ms. Petrelli had asked her how she did it, Murphy had explained that she and her dad ran several miles each afternoon. During that conversation, many of the students had volunteered comments about their families' physical activities. She remembered Brian had shared how his uncle had moved back to town and had been playing basketball with him. Ms. Petrelli had noticed that Brian's ball-handling skills had recently shown marked improvement and had pondered the reason. She remembered Kyle telling how he, Kevin, and Kathy all played soccer with the same league as their mom, and their dad had decided to take up the sport. The Carter family had always been involved in numerous sports sponsored by the city parks and recreation department.

"Yo, Ms. P., have you called about the bicycles yet?" Katie questioned as she plopped down onto the ground. As Ms. Petrelli turned her attention to Katie she smiled to herself at the familiarity with which Katie had addressed her, remembering how the nickname had come to pass. Most people assumed that Ms. P. was short for Ms. Petrelli. Actually, Ms. P. was short for Ms. P. E. When Katie was in kindergarten, she and her best friend Stephanie had been so excited about school. She wasn't exactly sure how the two little ones had confused P. E. and Petrelli, but the name had stuck and eventually shortened to Ms. P. over the years.

Katie was another one of Ms. Petrelli's students who voluntarily did little jobs for Ms. Petrelli. Katie had broken her ankle a couple of years back about the same time Ms. Petrelli had decided to reorganize her file cabinet, book shelves, and desk. Since Katie had been on crutches and a walking cast for close to two months, Ms. Petrelli had taken the time to teach her how she wanted everything reorganized. To this day Katie periodically stops by Ms. Petrelli's office and empties the purple "To Be Filed" basket kept on top of the file cabinet.

Nodding her head, Ms. Petrelli answered, "It looks like we will get the bikes in May." The bicycle safety program was originally sponsored and funded by the Women's Club. The purpose of the program was to teach fourth graders bicycle safety techniques such as correct stopping, proper hand signaling, and the rules of the road. The school district had requisitioned a school bus to transport a set of bicycles and additional instructional materials from school to school.

Looking up and noticing a few stragglers who had stopped to get a drink at the water fountain, Ms. Petrelli called out, "Let's go, you're holding us up." Ms. Petrelli considered whether or not she should remind the class of the water rule. After all, these students were such good workers that she bet they didn't even realize that they were thirsty until they stopped working.

As the stragglers approached, Ms. Petrelli directed, "Alright, let's review the overhand throwing pattern. What can you tell me?" As hands shot up around the group, several children began to call out responses. She found it amusing that there seemed to be an invisible string that connects a child's hand to their vocal cords; hands up, mouth in gear.

"Thank you for raising your hand, Autumn." Autumn had been sitting quietly and had not called out. She had a medium build with a square, chunky frame. Her light brown hair was cut in a page-boy style that accentuated her round face. She was not a high-energy child but demonstrated average skill level in most activities. Ms. Petrelli liked to call on her students who were not as skilled because she did not want any of her students thinking that physical education or physical activity was only for the highly skilled, athletic-type person.

Autumn replied, "Shoulder to your target, elbow back, ball by your ear. Umm . . . . extend your arm to your target and . . . " "NO! Step to your target," several students corrected, while several others called out "Point and release."

"Okay, Okay. Let's start again," Ms. Petrelli interjected. "Only this time, with someone demonstrating exactly what our bodies should be doing with each of our cues. Who would like to demonstrate?"

It was time to pick a boy because she had picked a girl last time. While working on her master's degree Ms. Petrelli had read about the hidden curriculum; how students subconsciously learn gender stereotypes. Thus, she purposely tried to call on an equal number of boys and girls in class, as well as tried to choose an equal number of boys and girls to demonstrate. In fact, she made a conscious effort to call on more boys to demonstrate or share with gymnastics and dance, and more girls to share or demonstrate with sports skills. She was very aware of and concerned about addressing the needs of diverse students, whether a gender, racial, or disability issue.

Observing the students seated before her wildly waving their hands, she asked, "David, will you be our demonstrator?" David was of average to low-average skill.

David's face immediately brightened as several students groaned their disappointment at not being chosen. David was of medium build with dark brown hair, sharp blue eyes, rosy cheeks, and a sprinkle of freckles across the bridge of his nose. He had only been at Glennview for a little over two years. During his first days in physical education he had seemed apprehensive and insecure. In fact he had gotten visibly upset and agitated on his first day because he didn't know how to jump rope. Ms. Petrelli remembered hugging him and explaining to him that his efforts were good. "Think how boring life would be if you already knew how to do everything and what a bummer it would be for me if I didn't have anything to teach you," she remembered telling him. To help David, Ms. Petrelli remembered calling on Kenny. Kenny, who was a little large for his age, was one of her highly skilled minority students. Best of all, he had a quiet, patient way of working and communicating with the other children. Ms. Petrelli had asked Kenny to take David to the physical education bathroom so he could wash his face and then teach him how to jump rope. Having her children feel good about their efforts in physical education was very important to her. She remembered how David left that day having had success jumping rope and how she had thanked Kenny for his help.

As David rose to demonstrate the overhand throwing pattern, Eddie and James started elbowing each other, giggling, and snickering. "Yeah, watch David, he throws just like a girl," singsonged James.

Ms. Petrelli watched David's face fall as several classmates laughed. She could feel the hairs on the back of her neck prickle and the heat rising to her face. As she bent over to pick up her clipboard she noticed her hands were trembling. As she sat down on a milk crate used for storing equipment, she thought, "Count to ten before you speak; don't let the children see how angry you are." But she could still feel the heat rising in her face and knew that her cheeks were turning pink.

As she glanced around at the children, those who had laughing faces were quickly sobering. Some of the children were looking at her anxiously, while others were looking down at their hands or had found a new absorbent interest in the grass. She knew from the children's expressions that the emotion she was experiencing was written all over her face. She needed to say or do something.

"Eddie, James, I think . . . " She paused—what did she think? What a cruel, hateful thing to say. How dare you purposely hurt another student, especially someone as kind and sensitive as David. But would time-out solve the problem? Or would they only learn not to express such statements out loud. Besides anger, she felt frustration. Where do these kids get this garbage? Where does it come from? Don't they realize that this is the 1990s? Boys, girls, blacks, whites have choices today. You can do whatever you choose. You can participate in any type of activity you want.

Choosing her words slowly and carefully almost through gritted teeth, she quietly asked, "Eddie, James, do you have something you would like to share?" Eddie lowered his head and looked at his hands mumbling, "I'm sorry, David." She wondered what Eddie was really sorry for. Was he sorry that he had hurt David's feelings or that he had made an obvious social faux pas? Or was he sorry that he was in trouble and might be punished? Even worse, Ms. Petrelli might call his dad and then he would be placed on restriction for sure. Eddie was basically a good kid, but he was a follower. He was easily swayed by the actions of others.

As she gazed at James he met her gaze directly, smirking and shrugging his shoulders. It was obvious that James wasn't sorry for anything. It dawned on her that she really didn't know James as well as she knew most of her other students. In the year and a half he had been at Glennview he had a high number of absences. She had never seen or met James's parents at any of the school functions, such as open house, P.T.O. ice cream socials, dinner theater musicals, spring festival, or field day.

There were so many issues at stake here. David's hurt feelings were only one of them. Of course, the children were not aware of all the underlying meanings communicated by statements such as "throws like a girl," or "runs like a girl."

As she agonized over the dilemma she remembered other instances that had transpired over the recent years. At the time they had seemed minute and trivial. Now she wondered. She recalled times when the older students had earned reward time or free time in class. It seemed that the boys almost always chose ball-type games or activities and the girls almost always chose tumbling or jump rope. Seldom did she remember observing a group of girls organizing a game of kickball, basketball, or soccer or the boys playing jump rope.

Come to think of it, what about some of the physical education written work and homework assignments? Again, the children seemed to depict themselves in very gender stereotypical roles, such as the last assignment when asked to draw a flipbook of an athlete in motion. Most of the boys had drawn male athletes playing basketball or football, while most of the girls had drawn female athletes jumping rope or tumbling.

Earlier in the year the students had been asked to cut out pictures of activities that improve cardiovascular endurance. Thinking back through the posters, she remembered the children had picked pictures of males in aggressive, powerful, action-oriented photographs and the female athletes were shown in graceful, flexible, ballet-like movements.

She now recalled several instances that before seemed incidental but now seemed significant. Like the way Ms. Smith divides her class into a boys' line and a girls' line when she picks them up after the physical education lesson, or how Ms. Jones seats her children in a boy-girl-boy-girl arrangement. What about the day that Sally and Jimmy collided on the playground during recess? Ms. Johnson had rushed over to pick Sally up and brush her off but had said very little to Jimmy.

As she slowly shook her head, feeling confused and perplexed, her frustration continued to mount. It isn't as if she had ignored gender stereotypes or had been blind. She had spent many an hour over the years making visual aids, bulletin boards, and huge theme displays depicting both boys and girls in a variety of activities. She had refused to use or hang commercially developed bulletin board sets that contained the male football player and the female cheerleader.

This was definitely one of those teachable moments, she thought, but how should she approach it? And if she decided to open Pandora's box, it was obvious that overhand throwing and catching would not be the day's focus. She was snapped back to the class seated before her when Lee asked, "Ms. Petrelli, are you okay?"

Questions
Preparing for Learning & Teaching

1. What is the critical issue in this case?

2. Who are the characters in the case?

3. What role did the characters play in creating/solving these issues?

4. What are some of the suggested strategies you might try to address these issues?

5. What does "throws like a girl" mean to you?

6. What are some strategies you could have used to intervene with the comment "throws like a girl"?

7. How would you have handled David's hurt feelings?

8. Should there have been any follow-up discipline for Eddie and/or James? If yes, cite examples. If no, explain why.

9. Do you think gender differences are biologically or socially constructed? Why?

10. Given that Ms. Petrelli seems to be committed to a gender-equitable program (curriculum choices, bulletin boards, and class procedures), why do you think this situation occurred?

11. What are some additional strategies you would suggest to provide for a more gender-equitable environment/program?

12. What additional ways can physical educators overcome gender bias?

13. How would you go about inservicing faculty and administration about underlying inequities at school?

14. How would you go about informing parents of unconscious gender bias?

15. Can you identify additional hidden school curricula or messages that are being taught in public education?

16. What are the related issues and questions raised by this case?

17. What are some of the specific elements that contribute to these issues (culturally learned gender biases, values, and/or prejudices)?

Cooperative Teaching Relationship

Luz Cruz

Sharon A. Varni

Case 16

The East Street School is a K–5 inner-city school in Massachusetts. It houses approximately 350 students, who are mostly Hispanic or African-American. Ms. Vincent, the physical education teacher at the school, takes great pride in how she has been able to develop the physical education program over the past four years. She describes her program as a skill themes program based on the movement framework. The limited facilities consist of a small indoor gymnasium (15' x 20') and a blacktop area that can be used, weather permitting. Despite the limited facilities and equipment, Ms. Vincent has gained much respect for her program from colleagues, administrators, parents, and students. Over the years, Ms. Vincent has continued to receive a budget, which has allowed her to acquire developmentally appropriate equipment to complement the goals and objectives she has set for her program. When Ms. Vincent agreed to supervise a student teacher from her old college, one of her concerns was that it would take a very "special" person to be able to perform successfully, given the limited space and equipment.

Ms. Kelly Jones was assigned to the East Street School for her elementary practicum experience. She'd had a very positive prepracticum experience and had her heart set on teaching at the elementary level upon graduation. Kelly felt that she was

> I was so nervous throughout the entire class that I felt as if my heart was going to burst right out of my chest. The funny thing is that I didn't feel that way until right before the class entered the gymnasium. I felt like Ms. Vincent was watching and judging my every move. After the class left, I noticed I was dripping with sweat.

very well prepared for student teaching due to the success she had in her methods courses. She had also heard many positive things about Ms. Vincent and her program.

Prior to the beginning of the school year, all of the teachers in the district had to attend an inservice workshop. Attending the inservice with Ms. Vincent gave Kelly an opportunity to get to know her better. Kelly found that Ms. Vincent had a great sense of humor, was easy to talk to, and appeared to be well liked and respected by her peers and administrators.

During the first few days of the semester, Kelly became familiar with Ms. Vincent's rules, expectations, and management techniques for the physical education classes. The review sessions, which Ms. Vincent conducted with her classes after their summer vacation, gave Kelly an idea of the content of the physical education program. Ms. Vincent set the tone for appropriate behavior in her classes and made it very clear that she would not tolerate inappropriate behavior. Kelly was informed about the rotational system—classes would have physical education three times per week for three weeks and then not again for three weeks. Knowing about the rotation made Kelly feel that it would be even harder for her to learn the students' names than she had anticipated.

Ms. Vincent appeared to be very relaxed with her approach to teaching and yet she was very strict. She liked to have fun with the students but also had very high expectations regarding behavior. Ms. Vincent had many incentives in place to motivate and/or reward students for proper behavior and on-task performance (e.g., Star Chart for first graders, Trade-in Tickets toward activity options for second grade, and Sneaker Beaders—beads to put on sneaker laces—for third through fifth grades). Kelly was impressed with what she saw and felt she was fortunate to have Ms. Vincent as her cooperating teacher.

The lessons that Kelly taught during the first two weeks of the semester were those planned by Ms. Vincent. Although this took some of the pressure off Kelly with regard to planning, she knew Ms. Vincent wanted the lessons to be implemented in the manner she expected them to occur. Since Ms. Vincent was a good and experienced teacher, Kelly interpreted this to mean that it was to be done just the way Ms. Vincent would do it herself. Kelly started to feel some pressure to be "just like Ms. Vincent."

Although things seemed to be going relatively well, Kelly decided to stop by her college supervisor's office just to "chat." She hinted that she was feeling some tension with regard to her role as a student teacher working with a teacher who has such high expectations. This concern did not come as a surprise to the supervisor because she had read the entries Kelly had put in her weekly journal. Kelly reflected on those entries:

> The first class I was going to teach was a first-grade class. Prior to the class, I had gone through everything on my list of reminders and in my lesson plan and it was timed perfectly, or so I thought. During the lesson, it seemed as though I rushed through everything. Although I had plenty of time to go over personal and general space, I spoke extremely fast (I suppose this was due to my nervousness). I was so nervous throughout the entire class that I felt as if my heart was going to burst right out of my chest. The funny thing is that I didn't feel that

way until right before the class entered the gymnasium. I felt like Ms. Vincent was watching and judging my every move. After the class left, I noticed I was dripping with sweat—great way to be first thing in the morning (chuckle).

The next day I was going to review personal and general space with the other first-grade class. Up to this point, none of the classes had a problem with the concept of personal space. I told the students in this class to walk forward and continue walking until they found their own space. They were to raise their hand when they thought they had found a good personal space where they were not touching anyone or anything else. I guess I had this horrified look on my face when every single child had walked straight ahead until they were right up against the wall because the next thing I knew, Ms. Vincent had jumped in and taken over. I believe I would have handled it, but Ms. Vincent beat me to it. The rest of the class period was spent reviewing personal and general space. Even Ms. Vincent was stressed out after this class. We laughed about it afterwards, but I will definitely remember that first-grade class and that children take you literally.

Kelly felt very comfortable with her supervisor, and throughout the semester she stopped by the campus unexpectedly or called her on the phone. Much about her experience was also documented in her weekly journals. It was starting to appear that there was some tension between Kelly and Ms. Vincent regarding expectations and the way things "should be done."

By the third week, Ms. Vincent asked Kelly if she would like to plan her own lessons. When Kelly answered with a resounding "yes," Ms. Vincent told her to plan the lessons for the movement concepts of effort, beginning with the concept of time. Kelly was excited yet anxious, but she knew that she was ready for the challenge!

On Monday morning, Kelly arrived at the school earlier than usual so that she could get the equipment ready and hang up some posters she was going to use to help demonstrate the concept of time. The first period of the day was a prep period for Ms. Vincent and Kelly during which time they discussed the plans for the day. As she set up the equipment and hung the posters she kept reassuring herself that she was definitely ready to teach the lessons that day. Ms. Vincent arrived, acknowledged the set-up, and then they sat down to discuss the lesson.

Ms. Vincent offered several suggestions for Kelly's lesson: "I can see that you put a lot of thought into the lesson plan, but I'm not sure it will work with these students. I have found that it is best to teach the concept by using music with different tempos rather than starting off using different pieces of equipment. I start them out by having them move different body parts to the music in personal space and then moving in general space. It's not until the second lesson that I may have them work with the equipment. These students will be so excited about using the different types of equipment that they will not be able to focus on the concept. Once they've had the opportunity to understand and use the concept, then I'll let them work with the equipment."

Kelly, caught a bit off guard, asked, "So, you don't think I should do this lesson?"

Ms. Vincent responded, "Well, the lesson is fine in terms of the information, but I don't think the methods will work."

"So what do you suggest, since the class will be here shortly?"

Ms. Vincent quickly responded by saying that she should cover the same information but should try it with the music, instead of the equipment. "I have the music right here so it really won't take much time to set it up."

Although Kelly was a bit unsure of the last-minute plans, she taught the lesson as Ms. Vincent had suggested. After the first class Kelly thought that the lesson was okay, but she felt that it would have been better if she had done what she had originally planned—and it would have been more fun. Kelly was not feeling great about having to change how she taught, but at the same time, she understood that Ms. Vincent's main concern was to make sure that the students understood the concept.

Kelly's journal entries and her informal conversations with her supervisor continued to address concerns she had about her identity as a student teacher. She wondered if Ms. Vincent would allow her to really be "the teacher," if only for a day? Couldn't she try her own ideas and learn from the mistakes? After all, there are many effective ways to present information. Ms. Vincent's way isn't the only way!

After watching Kelly teach a few classes, Ms. Vincent seemed to have become more comfortable with what she saw. Kelly, however, was not feeling as comfortable. She felt that she was being *allowed* to teach Ms. Vincent's classes and therefore felt pressured to teach *what* Ms. Vincent wanted her to teach and *how* she wanted her to do it. Ms. Vincent often jumped into Kelly's lesson in an attempt to clarify or reiterate what Kelly had told the class. Sometimes, in her attempt to clarify, Ms. Vincent's explanation or action was not quite what Kelly was trying to get across to the students. At times, the information was even contrary to what Kelly was thinking.

Kelly wished she could just teach her own lessons. She could appreciate that Ms. Vincent was just trying to make the lessons good for the students, but it certainly made it very difficult for her as the student teacher. Ms. Vincent jumped in whenever there was a behavior problem or if Kelly seemed to get stuck for a moment when explaining a task to the class. During one third-grade class, Kelly was trying to get the students to work together to create a game that used the skills they had just practiced (striking with a short-handled implement). One group of students was really involved with the game they had created, so when Kelly blew the whistle for them to stop and listen, they took a bit longer to respond. Ms. Vincent immediately told them to take a time-out until they remembered what to do when they heard the whistle. Kelly was really bothered by this.

> I would never have done that because I thought it was great that they were so engaged with the task. I kept hoping that with time she wouldn't feel the need to do this and would learn to trust that I could handle whatever arose, or would at least give me a chance to try to resolve it. Most of the time when Ms. Vincent did "butt in," I was about to say or do exactly what she said anyway. It's just

that her style is more rigid, tighter than mine. She wants students to respond totally and immediately. I'm comfortable with a little more flexibility, as long as the students are on-task and responsive.

Ms. Vincent kept apologizing for always jumping in and said she would try not to do it so often, but Kelly wondered if that was really possible. Kelly went home that night and couldn't stop thinking about the overall tension between them. It was very difficult to learn how to do something when there was someone looking over your shoulder all the time:

> How will I ever learn if I don't get some freedom? I'm so afraid of not doing things *right,* of not doing things *her way.* Yet how can I tell Ms. Vincent that I don't want so much input? Wouldn't she be insulted? I don't want her to back off completely because I know I need some help, and I don't want her to think that I think she's not a good teacher because she is a good teacher. But, I'm just not her—I have a different style!

One morning, for some unknown reason, Ms. Vincent told Kelly that maybe she had been giving her too much guidance. She was going to "disappear" for a large part of the day—meaning that she would not always stay in the class, although she would be nearby. Kelly felt relieved and grateful and was actually looking forward to the challenge. Gradually, Ms. Vincent did start to drift in and out of the gym during classes. Kelly found that the students responded a bit differently when Ms. Vincent wasn't in the class, but Kelly always felt capable of controlling behavior and getting through her lessons.

> The moment she left I started to feel much more relaxed, although I knew that she was within earshot, but it was still different, easier when she was not in the room. I think it's natural to feel this way and I think it has a lot to do with the fact that I knew she wanted things done a certain way—*her way!* I felt that I was supposed to be a miniature Ms. Vincent. I am looking forward to the future when I can run my own program in my own way—or at least find out what *my way* really means. This is not to say that I think her way is wrong, but I think that at times she comes down too hard on her students.

As the semester progressed, the students started to respond much better to Kelly and she was getting better at making her expectations clear. Kelly learned not to start to speak until she had the students' attention. Kelly considered herself much more lenient than Ms. Vincent but believed she was still able to control her classes. Whenever Ms. Vincent saw a student do something that she did not deem appropriate, she would immediately attempt to rectify the situation.

One day when Ms. Vincent had left the class, the lesson went so well "it was scary." All of the students were on-task, they did very well with the task, and it was one of those classes when Kelly felt it couldn't have gone any better! Ms. Vincent had been listening to the class (standing outside the room) and had agreed. "What a great feeling!" Kelly thought. Everything continued to go well when Ms. Vincent wasn't present in the classes—until that one fifth-grade period:

The students were having an especially bad day, where they were not respect-ing each other and had terrible attitudes. I had to stop and talk to the entire group about their behavior. I even threatened them by saying that if their behav-ior didn't improve they would not have physical education. Ms. Vincent poked her head out of the window (we were outside on the blacktop) and asked how things were going, to which I just shook my head. Ms. Vincent was outside in less than ten seconds, and she echoed everything that I had already said. At that point, I wasn't sure how I was feeling about her coming to the rescue. Do I wish she had left me to figure it out? Or, was I glad she was there, although she really wasn't able to do much more than what I had done? I guess for the most part, it was just good to feel that I was not alone.

Over the next couple of meetings with the same fifth-grade class, it seemed that the students were once again willing and able to cooperate with Kelly. She found that the kindergartners were the most difficult group for her. She had not had much prior experience working with that level. Although Kelly didn't always appreciate when Ms. Vincent inter-rupted her classes, the kindergartners were a different story. With this group, Ms. Vincent's interference was sometimes very helpful and appro-priate. One day Kelly started to teach one of the kindergarten classes and about ten minutes into the lesson Ms. Vincent took over. Kelly thought:

> I didn't think the lesson was going too badly, but the younger students had a way of "frazzling" me. The look on my face probably led her to believe that I needed help. It bothered me a bit, and yet I felt that maybe I wasn't ready for the K classes. I kept thinking—maybe by next week . . . .

Overall, Kelly felt that things were going well. The students contin-ued to respond to her in a positive way, and she felt that she was doing a good job planning and implementing lessons (although she always shared her ideas for the lessons with Ms. Vincent prior to teaching them). Ms. Vincent started to trust Kelly to plan and manage the classes and pro-vide a safe learning environment for the students. Even the fifth-grade class that had given her some trouble earlier on had come around. They had become receptive to Kelly's lessons and her expectations. One day while she was doing recess duty, one of the fifth graders came to her to tell her that the students had been talking and saying that they enjoyed having her as a teacher and they were learning a lot. That single com-ment made every doubtful moment seem worthwhile!

The next time she met that fifth-grade class for physical education she was pretty psyched because they had validated her as a teacher. Ms. Vincent looked at the lesson plan and commented that although it was different than what *she* would do, it would be okay for Kelly to try it anyway. She warned Kelly to make sure that she emphasized the safety issues she had listed in the plan.

Kelly explained to the class that the focus of the lesson was weight transfer. She told them that it was important for them to understand this concept because it is something that is used when playing different sports. After she explained the focus of the lesson, she had them get into groups of four, and each group had to work at one of the folded mats (folded to be about 16" thick, approximately 5' long and 2' wide). Kelly emphasized safety, and especially, how to share the mat. The students were challenged with a variety of tasks (e.g., see if you can transfer your weight from two feet on the floor to one foot onto the mat and maintain your balance for three seconds; how might you transfer your weight from two feet on the floor to another body part across the mat?). Kelly was moving around the room and giving individual feedback to different groups when she heard a student screaming that his arm was hurt. Kelly ran over to the student immediately. "David, what's the matter, what happened?"

"Michael jumped on the mat while I was still there and he landed on one foot but he landed on my arm. Ouch, it hurts so much!"

"Tina, please run up to the nurse's office and tell her to come here right away. The rest of you get away from David. Go sit on the line! David will be alright."

The three to four minutes Kelly waited for the nurse seemed like hours. She spent that time hoping that David was going to be all right and trying to figure out what had happened and why. She kept asking herself what she had done or not done to allow this to happen. What would happen when Ms. Vincent comes back? Where was she, anyway? Usually she was there even when I didn't need her to be, but now she wasn't. What would she think? Ms. Vincent arrived just before the nurse showed up. She ran right over to the mat where Kelly and David were sitting. She asked, "What happened? How did it happen?" The other students all had something to say, but Ms. Vincent was only looking at Kelly and David and waiting for a response.

Name   Date

Questions
Preparing for Learning & Teaching

1. What is the critical issue in this case?

2. What are some of the possible tensions that may exist between cooperating teachers and student teachers?

3. How important is a positive relationship between the cooperating teacher and the student teacher?

4. Do you think you could have a positive student teaching experience without a good relationship? Explain your response.

5. Overall, how would you describe the relationship between Ms. Vincent and Kelly Jones?

6. To what extent do you believe that the lines of communication between Ms. Vincent and Kelly were open?

7. Why do you think Kelly never told Ms. Vincent about how she felt about her "jumping in"?

8. What would you do if you found yourself in a similar situation?

9. If you were Kelly, would you have approached Ms. Vincent about wanting to try different things in different ways? Why? If you approached her, how/when would you do it?

10. Do you think it is ever appropriate for the cooperating teacher to "jump in"? Please explain your response.

11. What would you have liked/expected from a student teacher in this situation? Why?

12. What would you have liked/expected from a cooperating teacher in this situation? Why?

13. What would you have liked/expected from a university supervisor in this situation?

14. What are the related issues and questions raised by this case?

15. What strategies might you use to address these issues?

Case studies in physical
education : real world
preparation for teaching